Twayne's United States Authors Series

Sylvia E. Bowman, *Editor*

INDIANA UNIVERSITY

Djuna Barnes

TUSAS 262

Courtesy of Farrar, Straus and Cudahy

Djuna Barnes

DJUNA BARNES

By JAMES B. SCOTT
University of Bridgeport

TWAYNE PUBLISHERS
A DIVISION OF G. K. HALL & CO., BOSTON

First Printing

Library of Congress Cataloging in Publication Data

Scott, James B.
Djuna Barnes.

(Twayne's United States authors series ; TUSAS 262)
Bibliography:pp.148–50.
Includes index.
1. Barnes, Djuna.
PS3503.A614Z9 818'.5'209 [B] 75-45214
ISBN 0-8057-7153-0

MANUFACTURED IN THE UNITED STATES OF AMERICA

This book is for all my women friends, and my wife

Contents

About the Author

Professor James B. Scott has published articles on Robert Penn Warren and Theodore Dreiser, and a study guide to William Golding's *Lord of the Flies.* He is preparing for publication a new study of Henry James' *The Turn of the Screw.* He has taught American literature for twenty-two years, and has for at least half that time included *Nightwood* in his upper level and graduate courses.

Professor Scott received his B.A. and M.A. degrees from the University of Buffalo and his Ph.D. from Syracuse University. Since 1964 he has taught American literature at the University of Bridgeport.

Preface

Djuna Barnes's stories do not appear in anthologies of American fiction; nor are her poems reprinted in poetry collections. Scholarly surveys of American literature fail even to index her name. The following study is partially anachronistic; it is addressed to readers who for the main part have yet to read the works herein discussed. Miss Barnes belongs (to speak in classifications) in that generation of expatriated artists quartered in Paris during the 1920's and commonly known as the Lost Generation. I do not regard these writers as having been at all lost — on the contrary, Western society had itself become lost, and that slender coterie comprised one of the few groups which so understood matters. Such identifications with "generations" or "schools" however, are not of true relevance in any case, for Djuna Barnes's writing reaches far beyond the topical. Above all, she is a stylist, an innovator and even an inventor of literary language. Indeed, as will be shown, her most imaginative efforts look both backward to a vocabulary old-to-archaic, as well as forward, to constantly reinvent a language, challenging in its metaphors and images, yet at once precise and elegant. Perhaps "unexpected" best describes the versatility of her writing. Her literary efforts are her endorsement, if not of a world gone wrong, at least of the worthiness of the artistic expression of those wrongs.

Miss Barnes's first novel, *Ryder*, has been out of print since 1928; *Ladies Almanack* (from the same year) was reissued in 1974 (by Harper and Row), after an elapse of 46 years. *A Book* (1928) revised as *A Night Among the Horses* (1929) has been long out of print. Yet these last two titles encompass subtly written, frequently profound, stories, eleven Imagist poems, and three one-act plays written in the then new Realistic manner. One of these plays. *Three From the Earth*, appeared, during the 1919–1920 season of the infant Provincetown Playhouse, on the same bill with Eugene O'Neill's *The*

Dreamy Kid. A season vital to the birthing of modern American theater, it ushered in a formidable new drama with O'Neill, its mentor and chief innovator. Miss Barnes's *Three From the Earth,* a detailed portrayal of a woman, not as a type but as an individual, and written within the mode of the new Realism, was not understood by critics as capable as Alexander Woollcott when it was originally performed. Miss Barnes insists upon her highly personal vision of life as suffering and loss; moreover, she characteristically "distances" herself from her characters, who, in turn, live solely within their own subjectivity. Achieving the author's point of view or the "meaning" of Barnes's works thus demands an attention and commitment far enough beyond the ordinary to be unexpected. Her works *can* be understood—with effort.

In 1962, the publication of *The Selected Works of Djuna Barnes* made partial correction of the above oversight; it included *Nightwood, The Antiphon,* and nine stories. However, many of Barnes's stories, as well as the eleven poems and three one-act plays mentioned previously are still not available.

Miss Barnes's one attempt at a "popular" novel, *Nightwood,* (1936) continues to be both admired and influential. T. S. Eliot, who wrote the preface to that novel found, twelve years later, that he had no occasion, in prefacing the second edition, to change his original praise of this work of "creative imagination". In his note to the second edition (included in *The Selected Works of Djuna Barnes*) he wrote, "As my admiration for the book has not diminished, and my only motive for revision would be to remove or conceal evidences of my own immaturity at the time of writing—a temptation which may present itself to any critic reviewing his own words at twelve years' distance—I have thought best to leave unaltered a preface which may still, I hope, serve its original purpose of indicating an approach which seems to me helpful for the new reader". Eliot's praise of *Nightwood* has been shared by enthusiastic readers, students, scholars and writers since 1936. Sadly, that novel is the only work by Barnes most people have ever read.

Acknowledgments

I first became interested in Miss Barnes's writing through Professor David Owen, at Syracuse University. Since then, I have become further indebted to many students, through class discussions and papers, for insights which I have assimilated and now take for my own. Librarians at the Beinecke Library, Yale University, New Haven, the Bridgeport Public and the University of Bridgeport libraries, the 42nd Street Research Library and the Jefferson Market Branch of the New York Public Library, as well as librarians in several public and university libraries have universally responded to my requests. Although I do not know their names, I thank them all. I am especially grateful for the research and manuscript assistance given me by Daria Lewis.

Chronology

1892 June 12, Djuna Barnes, born at Cornwall-on-Hudson, New York; daughter of Wald and Elizabeth (Chappell) Barnes. Educated at home. Studied painting at Pratt Institute and at the Art Students' League.

1913 Reporter-illustrator for Brooklyn *Eagle*; subsequently worked for many New York newspapers.

1913–1931 Began publishing short stories. First stories accepted by *Munsey's*, Sunday *Telegraph*, *Little Review*, *All-Story* magazine. *Smart Set*, *Dial*, and *Vanity Fair* (in which she used the pseudonym, Lydia Steptoe). Wrote articles and, for a time, a column for *Theatre Guild Magazine*.

1915 *The Book of Repulsive Women* published in New York by [Guido] Bruno Chapbook. Several pieces accepted by *All-Story* and *Dial*; somewhat later by *Smart Set*, and *McCall's*.

1919–1920 Associated with Provincetown Players who produced three of her one-act plays *Kurzy of the Sea*, *Three From the Earth*, and *Irish Triangle*.

1920 Went abroad on commission for *McCall's* to write interviews.

1923 *A Book* published by Horace Liveright.

1925 Represented in *Contact Collection of Contemporary Writers*, a sampling of works in progress published in Paris by Three Mountains Press.

1926 *The Dove* produced by Samuel Eliot of Smith College at the Studio Theatre.

1928 *Ryder* published by Boni and Liveright.

1928 *Ladies Almanack* printed privately and anonymously by "A Lady of Fashion."

1929 *A Night Among the Horses* (a reissue of *A Book* with three stories added) published by Liveright.

1936 *Nightwood* published in London by Faber and Faber.

1937 *Nightwood* published in New York by Harcourt Brace.
1943 *Alice*, painted in 1934, is exhibited at Art of This Century Gallery in New York.
1958 *The Antiphon* published in London by Faber and Faber; in New York by Farrar, Straus & Cudahy.
1961 *The Antiphon*, produced by Royal Theatre in Stockholm, translated by Dag Hammerskköld and Karl Ragnar Gierow. Trustee, New York Commission of Dag Hammerskköld Foundation; member, National Institute of Arts and Letters.
1962 *The Selected Works of Djuna Barnes* published in New York by Farrar, Straus and Cudahy.
1962 *Spillway* published in London by Faber and Faber.
1969 "The Quarry" published by *The New Yorker*.
1971 "The Walking-Mort" published by *The New Yorker*.
1972 *Ladies Almanack* published in New York by Harper & Row.
1972 *Spillway* published in New York by Harper & Row.
1974 *Vagaries Malicieux* published in New York by Frank Hallman.

CHAPTER 1

Early Life

DJUNA BARNES was born on June 12, 1892 in a chalet on Storm-King Mountain near Cornwall-on-Hudson, New York. Her father, Wald Barnes, was an American; her mother, Elizabeth Chappell Barnes, British. After Wald Barnes met his wife-to-be in England (where he had gone with his mother, Zadel Barnes), he brought Elizabeth Chappell to America and married her. The family's wanderings took them to Cornwall-on-Hudson, Fordham, and later to a hundred-and-five-acre farm on Long Island where the undeveloped condition of that part of New York State lent itself to Wald Barnes's desire for a life of independence from society, for privacy, and for creativity. He was equipped for such a life: he could fix most anything; he built his own house; plowed and planted his fields; and slaughtered his own pigs and chickens. He wrote his own "Credo," a literary statement of the beliefs he followed in shaping his life.

Djuna Barnes was educated at home by Zadel Barnes, her grandmother, an early feminist and a teacher, who lived with the family. Miss Barnes's education reflected not family affluence but family agreement that what the public schools offered its pupils was inadequate and in some ways even detrimental to a child's development. Learning was an intensely ongoing process in the family, but even more important than the sessions at reading and writing was the atmosphere of dedication to the arts inspired by Wald and Zadel. In the evenings, Zadel Barnes, seated by the fire often read aloud from a wide spectrum of authors. Music was also important, since Wald Barnes was accomplished enough to play the piano, as well as several other instruments; moreover, he composed operas and wrote his own libretti. Miss Barnes learned to play the banjo, the violin, and the French horn. The visual arts were encouraged as well; Wald Barnes could paint a good watercolor, and his oldest daughter was to become an accomplished artist as well as illustrator. The life of the family was close, and each of the family's varied interests contributed its own educational dimensions: the explicitly literary and artistic activities, the formal lessons, and even the daily processes of gathering a living from the land. Miss Barnes, something of a tomboy, helped work the farm; she played with her brothers; and, from an early age, she liked to write poetry, to act, and even to construct little plays.

In many ways Wald Barnes was a gifted man and one of vision. He trusted nature but distrusted society; and he had an unbounded confidence in his own rightness. He rejected his father and even his surname, Buddington, in preference to his mother's name, Barnes. Mother and son, as can be seen, were so close that they shared a common philosophy. Wald Barnes's rebelliousness was shaped by his refusal to live by the conventions of late-Victorian society and by his messianic impulse to reform that society to the prototype of nature herself. But, when he learned that his naturalistic vision set him in automatic conflict with the codes of his time, he chose the way of independence. He became a quasi-farmer, and he created about himself an almost entirely self-sufficient family unit.

As a young woman, Miss Barnes studied at Pratt Institute and at the Art Students League. Her first employment was as a newspaperwoman and illustrator for the Brooklyn *Eagle*, and her stories and Imagist poems began to appear in a number of periodicals. Her earliest fiction, the stories collected in *A Book*, makes use of American settings in which appear central characters who are in some way alien to the American scene. Sometimes they are native born, but most often they are immigrants from European countries. Most of her primary characters are women, while men usually appear in only secondary roles.

By the time Miss Barnes joined the Provincetown Players for the 1919–1920 season, she was already a published poet and short story writer. Her *Three From the Earth* appeared on the same evening's bill with a premiere performance of Eugene O'Neill's *The Dreamy Kid*. That landmark season, which brought both Miss Barnes and O'Neill to public attention, was enriched as well with the premieres of two other Barnes one-act plays, *Kurzy of the Sea*, and *Irish Triangle*. At the end of that season, Miss Barnes left for Europe to write and interview famous personalities for *McCall's* magazine. Two years later, in 1922, James Joyce's *Ulysses* was published by

Shakespeare and Company, and T. S. Eliot's *The Waste Land* also appeared. By this time, Miss Barnes knew both Joyce and Eliot well and was close friends with Robert McAlmon (of Contact Editions). She knew Ezra Pound, William Carlos Williams, Gertrude Stein, and many other expatriate writers and artists who were forming the nucleus of what was to be a decade of such lively and intense Paris-based artistic creativity that it has not since been equalled.

The 1920s was an innovative but also introspective decade for writers who were usually thoroughly disillusioned with their world. Its enormous hatreds had erupted into World War I. Then the war's aftermath of greed and corruption, the fiasco of the Versailles Treaty, and the crass materialism of entire nations, America especially, wore away whatever idealism might have survived the war itself. The writers of this decade, possessed of enormous talent, lacked hopeful real-life models. They were faced with essentially three choices: they could write naturalistically about the actualities of this violent century; they could begin looking backward for their models; or they could try to do both. The best writers, typified by Joyce, Eliot, and Miss Barnes, began to follow a double vision which imposed a nostalgia for man's heritage, as well as his ability to believe in, and to hope for, the actualities of a here-and-now real world.

This sense of the past is stylistically melded into Barnes's *Ryder*, *Ladies Almanack* and *The Antiphon* through literary borrowings, allusions and parody. Even works which seem more "modern" in their language (like her stories and like *Nightwood*) retain a thematic tension between the longed-for certainties of the past, and an unpalatable present. Eliot and Joyce revealed themselves (as did Pound) as consciously literary in their major works, for both *Ulysses* and *The Waste Land* derive in fairly direct fashion from many sources. *The Waste Land* owes its slight plot and its rich allusions to many sources, including the legend of the fisher king, the Holy Grail, Wagner, Mother Goose, the New Testament, and the *Chanson de Roland*. Many of its lines are fragments taken from other works without benefit of quotes (affirming, perhaps, Eliot's dictum that lesser poets plagiarize but that great poets *steal*!), but the fragments that Eliot appropriated had a great deal to do with his artistic purpose. He wanted to contrast modern man's predicament with earlier times when, through the metamorphoses of art and religion, it was possible to transform the ugly and meaningless into forms of beauty and redemption. Nostalgia and a longing for religious certitude have much to do with the success of *The Waste Land*. For his poem to accomplish its purposes, Eliot had to remind his readers of their heritage; therefore, his "borrowings" can be justified.

In *Ulysses* Joyce attempted an even bolder, although again derivative, object. Many styles are employed in that novel which looks at a single day in the lives of certain characters living in Dublin in a very real twentieth century. The narrative adopts as a framework the model of *The Odyssey*, against which the episodes in *Ulysses* are juxtaposed. Ulysses's dalliance with the nymph Nausicaa, for example, suggested mythic man's relationship to the eternal in forms of beauty in a sexual context that was flattering to Homer's contemporaries. In Joyce's use of the Homeric incident, Bloom is no more than a *voyeur* observing young Gerty MacDowell perched on the rocks as she bends backwards seductively on the pretext of watching the fireworks. This scene is a cheap and thrilling one for both participants, yet there can be no question that Joyce created Gerty with love and compassion and Bloom with admiration and respect. *Ulysses* presents in artistic form a counterpart to ultimate cheapness—life itself. Joyce, then, told a contemporary tale by inviting comparisons with Homer and other writers to describe the irrecoverable distance man has traveled from his antecedent cultural veracities. Stylistically, Joyce, who tried to suit the content to the form, borrowed freely from the styles of John Bunyan, Jonathan Swift, Thomas Malory; the sentimental novelists; and many others. Moreover, he parodied not only these older styles but those of writers of his own day.

These illustrations suggest the desire among writers of the 1920s for affirmations not to be found in the real world (Hemingway would later skirt the issue in *The Sun Also Rises* by writing his own rules for an "in" society which operated by its own code of manners in its own self-defined realities). Unlike Barnes, both Eliot and Joyce were determined enough, in fact, to weld positive hopes and conclusions to their works. Whether those are justified hopes is not germane in this discussion. What is important to notice is the derivative quality of their work—their felt-necessity for looking backward which appeared in the works of these literary giants.

Miss Barnes was in close contact with associates self-consciously literary to even an esoteric extent; and she was reaching toward maturity as a writer. Among the literary influences cited as having informed Miss Barnes's work are such sources as the Bible, Geoffrey Chaucer, John Donne, John Milton, Joyce, Eliot, the Elizabethans and the Jacobeans. To this list might well be added the impetus of the short-lived Imagist movement. To state that Miss Barnes was influenced in various works by such various sources is only to say that she was developing her craftsmanship along lines being followed, at that time, by major writers of her acquaintance. Such recognition of influences is only partially helpful, however, for Miss Barnes's writing is of such widely varying styles as to make it apparent that some other criteria must be used to account for her amazing variety.

Her short stories are written in a tersely simple style. Her first and second novels, *Ryder* and *Ladies Almanack*, are clearly derivative in style, although each differs from the other. The mock-epic, *Ryder*, parodies many writers, while *Ladies Almanack* parodies eighteenth-century literature of Manners. Her most successful novel, *Nightwood*, is a unique modern work that is stylistically pure, unself-conscious, and not visibly affected by any derivative qualities. Miss Barnes's early poetry is decidedly Imagistic, and her late poetry still retains Imagist characteristics. Her verse-drama, *The Antiphon*, returns the reader to that literary world and its models—particularly Shakespeare and the Jacobean—from which she departed so dramatically in *Nightwood*.

The stylistic variety of her work is further complicated by the presence in a number of her works of a dimly recognizable authorial voice attributable to a persona of the author herself. This voice takes on stylistic alterations to suit the works in which it appears and the age and condition of the character. It is the voice of a young Julie in *Ryder*; of a young woman, Patience Scalpel, in *Ladies Almanack*; and of a woman in her fifties in the Miranda of *The Antiphon*. My approach in this study is to regard style and form both as variable modes designed, quite consciously, to suit the demand of the particular work; meanwhile, the "meaning" the work imparts is largely directed by form and style. *Nightwood*'s poetic yet simple style—its frequent colloquialisms and informal contemporary language—suggests the uniqueness of the tale told, as well as its timeless applicability. The Shakespearean overtones of *The Antiphon* invite comparison with an earlier literature and hence with an earlier time; thus content, form, and style are all variables. There are no constants at all; the work of art is generated at a certain creative heat which fuses style, form, and intent together to produce meaning. The ultimate desired effect, then, is a work which meets the author's initial intent, and all variables must give place to that ultimate achievement.

Miss Barnes's views about the subject of artistic creation are extremely uncompromising. She entirely rejects the impulse to "rush into print" with her latest piece of writing. To her, an artist has no business publishing everything he writes; instead, he creates because as artist he must; he is driven to creativity. But he should show the world only his very best work—and only a little of even that. For the artist must remain exclusive, free, private; his only commitment must be to the demands of such art. To Miss Barnes, the artist may not sell himself to the world and retain his own standards. Art to her is not a part of the consumer culture, a product to be mass produced and placed in the hands of every wage-earner. It cannot be expected that very many readers will appreciate the workmanship of fine art, so there is no reason to anticipate its wide circulation.

Miss Barnes's attitude toward the "market," the reading public with a taste for literature, was fixed as early as the final issue of *The Little Review* in 1929 when she refused to answer any questions at all about herself, or about her opinions of world or artistic issues; indeed, she flatly stated her lack of respect for "the public."[1] These postulates of Miss Barnes's esthetics are visibly related to her philosophical stance—one so consistently apparent throughout her writing—that the entire human enterprise is an atrocious but alluring mistake. Never to have been born at all would be the highest good; having been born, to die quickly would be the next preference. Instead, to the artist's dismay, men fall (very understandably) in love with women who reciprocate; the expression of their love generates more births and hence more deaths. And, to compound the error, life itself is filled with pain, anguish, loneliness, and suffering of every imaginable kind; therefore, even if the life-death cycle could be justified, or at least accepted with equanimity, a person is still faced with the irresolvable fact that his journey is not worth the ride.

As might be presumed, Miss Barnes's works are profoundly concerned with the most trying questions known to man; and even her lightest stories rest upon the firm foundation of her despair. Just as the setting is important to her work, just as her characters are so consistently alienated from the places in which they are found, so place has a visible effect upon the creative process of molding the form, style, and intent used by the author. Her earliest stories, set in rural America and in New York City, reflect her own upbringing and emergence into her urban life as a reporter-illustrator. Her first novel, *Ryder*, uses the rural New York setting of her own childhood. The later stories, which appeared in *A Night Among the Horses*, reflect her residence in Europe and chiefly in Paris. *Ladies Almanack* is set in Paris; *Nightwood* is set mainly in Paris, but it also shows scenes in Berlin, a city with which the author was familiar, and ends in the rural upstate New York setting so reminiscent of Cornwall-on-Hudson, or the Long Island farm. *The Antiphon*—with its flight from occupied Paris to England, and with its World War II background an integral part of the setting—reminds us of Miss Barnes's own last-minute flight in 1940 from Europe to America by way of England. We might speculate that Miss Barnes's own experiences with the world have from first to last reinforced in her a sense not only of her own but of all mankind's essential isolation in the self; and this alienation from the world has never made anyone very comfortable.

CHAPTER 2

A Book, A Night Among the Horses *and* Spillway

A BOOK, published in 1923, is a collection of twelve stories, three one-act plays, eleven poems, and a half-dozen pencil portraits. Most of this material had appeared in various magazines, notably in *Harper's, The New Republic,* and *Dial;* but quite a number had been published in *The Little Review* with which Miss Barnes was for a time closely associated. *A Night Among the Horses and Other Stories* (1929) is a reprint of *A Book* with the addition of three stories: "Aller et Retour," "A Little Girl Tells a Story to a Lady," and "The Passion." *Spillway* (1962), which collects nine stories, contains eight from *A Night* and one, "The Grande Malade," from Ford Madox Ford's *Transatlantic Review* where it was first printed under the title "The Little Girl Continues." The nine stories of *Spillway,* which are readily available in the *Selected Works of Djuna Barnes* (1962), were reedited by Miss Barnes for that edition.

All of the material in *A Book* reflects the American milieu, and the stories added to *A Night* are presented against a European background. This change reflects Miss Barnes's nine-years' residence in Europe prior to the 1929 publication of *A Night Among the Horses;* and this circumstance is of more than biographical importance since setting matters a great deal in Barnes's work. The characters in *A Book* are frequently immigrants to America, and even those who are not have names suggestive of their European origins. Many are Russians; some are a mixture of Jewish and European strains. They have heavily ethnic names like the Germanic Emma Gonsberg, Julie Anspacher, Helena Hucksteppe, Freda Buckler; Irish names like Kate Morley; Russian like Vera Sovna, Katrina Silverstaff (her husband a Jew); French, Nelly

Grissard. Rugo Amietiev, an Armenian, has come to New York, as has his Italian girl friend, Addie; also from Italy comes Carmen la Tosca.

These names reveal something of the author's purpose, for her characters' expatriated condition offers a natural symbol for man's essential aloneness. This same principle of using expatriated characters to suggest aloneness or alienation is continued in the European stories added to *A Night Among the Horses.* Erling von Bartmann, a Russian widow, lives in Paris in "Aller et Retour"; but the story begins with Madame at Marseilles, and the action occurs in the outskirts of Nice. The narrator of "Cassation" is Russian; Gaya in that story is Italian; her husband, German; the action described occurred in Berlin; but the narrator is in Paris when she tells about it. Katya, the narrator of "The Grande Malade," and her sister Moydia are also Russian; their grandmother was a Jew; and they have lived in Norway, Holland, and Paris. Moydia goes to Germany for a visit, and at the end of the story the sisters are planning to go to a different country, possibly America. Almost all significant characters in Barnes' stories have come from somewhere other than where they now live; and, of the remaining natives, these can justifiably be said to be strangers alienated from their own lands.

I *Characteristics of Barnes's Stories*

With the exception of "Cassation" and "The Grande Malade," Miss Barnes uses an impersonal third-person narrative technique. These two stories are told in the first person, and both are "framed" as stories within stories. In these two, a teenage girl entertains a slightly older woman, who is apparently an American and apparently a persona for Miss Barnes herself, while the two are seated in a cafe. At the end of the narration, the frame is "closed" by returning to the present location of the story, the cafe. Other than her role as auditress, Miss Barnes never appears as a character in her stories. The style of her stories is remarkably consistent. Naturalistic techniques are used throughout, but they are imposed upon an existential point of view. For want of a better term, I call this writing inverted naturalism. As is characteristic of naturalism, Miss Barnes employs an objective, almost indifferent tone; but her tone is varied occasionally, just as it is in the introduction of the young girl narrator, Katya, in "Cassation" and in the "The Grande Malade." Miss Barnes's style is sprightlier, as befits her narrator's youth and enthusiasm; but it is also varied because of the author's own sense of humor as it appears in the comedic situations of "The Robin's House," "A Boy Asks a Question of a Lady," "The Grande Malade," and "The Rabbit."

Nevertheless, humor is used sparingly and does not detract from the usually serious situations. In fact, the humor tends more clearly to provide the perspective which the author seeks to convey. Ultimately, life appears to be senseless and as even meaningless in Barnes's stories, and her touches of humor lend themselves to that attitude. In her treatment of life's meaning, we see the difference between naturalism of the kind Miss Barnes writes and existentialism. Despite the hard realism of naturalism, its determinism and its pessimistic outlook about man's ability to shape the world to his will, naturalistic writing nevertheless insists that human life can be rationally understood. Life is frequently tragic and painful, it is true; but the purpose of the naturalist is to show, nevertheless, *how* and *why* life is tragic and painful. The naturalist believes, that is, in the capability of logic and reason to understand life, even though he or his characters may be powerless to alter its hard realities.

Existentialism, on the other hand, posits not only that life is frequently tragic and painful but that life is also irrational. Some existentialists, like Jean Paul Sartre and Bertrand Russell, endow man with free will and urge him to make sensible patterns of his own within the larger frame of a meaningless universe. Miss Barnes sees life and the perpetuation of life as a mistake; indeed, the mistake is to be alive, and then by procreation, to compound that error and produce more tragedy and pain. She finds death, then, to be an affirmation and a triumph. Tragedy is not dying; rather, it is living. The meaninglessness and irrationality of life, she indicates, can be understood; for, put most simply—and paradoxically—the meaninglessness of life lies precisely in its meaning.

The term inverted naturalism describes, therefore, writing which is essentially positive even though the usual associations between life and hope versus death and despair (or tragedy) have been reversed. To describe Miss Barnes as an existentialist would be to suggest that she sees life as ultimately beyond understanding; but to do so is not accurate since she sees life as meaningless but as quite understandable. In the deepest sense, her stories can be said to show *how* and *why* death can be the only real affirmation in a meaningless universe.

As might be supposed, death is present in nearly every story, and is implicit in even the few lighter, more humorous ones. Romantic love is nonexistent in Barnes's stories, for physical attraction between the sexes draws men and women together. Love may appear between servant and master, as in "The Nigger"; between mother and child, as in "Cassation"; between wife and husband as in "The Doctors"; or between an engaged couple, as in "Indian Summer." But the love Katrina feels for her husband in "The Doctors" more closely resembles esteem, respect, or admiration; for her feeling for him is insufficient to prevent Katrina's suicide. The love Madame Boliver experiences in "Indian Summer" is the culmination of her rise in the whirl of social excitement and of her long delayed acceptance and admiration by a society which had ignored her for half a century. Her death leaves her fiancé irritated, rather than distraught.

Male characters appear most frequently in secondary roles. John in "A Night Among the Horses" and Rugo Amietiev in "The Rabbit" are her only two central male characters, yet even in these stories women become the shaping forces in the lives of the men: John is brought by a woman to his death; Rugo, to marriage. The remaining stories focus upon central female characters of a wide range in age, background, nationality, social and worldly success, and even wisdom. In these narratives, men are shown to be occasionally useful to women as fathers of their children and perhaps as their breadwinners; but men are not shown to be shaping forces in the lives of the female characters. Ultimately, men are used by women as their need presents itself; for women are frequently autonomous and strong willed.

II *The Epiphany*

Miss Barnes's stories move with the inevitable determinism of the naturalist toward their conclusions, but the conclusions are frequently enigmatic or ambiguous. Some of her characters know more at this point than they knew at the beginning of the events the story recounts, and others do not. The stories, that is, ultimately concern themselves with enlightening the reader rather than the characters. Madame La Tosca in "A Boy Asks a Question of a Lady" knows as much about puberty's mysteries at the start of the story as she does at the end, and the boy is not really enlightened by his encounter with her. John, the hostler in "A Night Among the Horses," dies in confusion; and he cannot be said to have made as much sense of his own life as the reader is invited to do. The concluding action of the stories may be as dramatic as the trampling to death of John in "A Night" or as slight a gesture as old Rabb's lifting her eyes a bit higher after Hardaway's death in "The Nigger" or as Moydia's new fashion in "The Grande Malade" of sugaring her tea from a greater height, now that she has become "tragique."

Obviously, the degree of finality of the concluding action serves as an index of the seriousness of the writing, and even the seriousness of the loss, when death concludes the story. The devices used to conclude the stories resemble James Joyce's epiphanies, but Miss Barnes's are fused with the conventional dramatic climax. The stories end in an action, or a gesture, the force of which is aimed at the reader and invites the reader's understanding. The epiphany, as Joyce conceived it, was a moment of illumination for the reader, which might or might not be shared by the character. For Joyce, it was not necessarily the most dramatic moment of his story; and it did not have to occur at the end of the narration, although it frequently did. Wherever it occurred, it was the moment when the forces of the story came into sharpest focus; and at that moment the reader could see most clearly what the various details had been pointing to from the beginning.

In Barnes's stories, the enlightenment tends to occur at the very end, often in the last sentence, and has some form of action or gesture which is intended to evoke in the reader one or more possibilities for grasping the significance of the events of the story. Since life, existence itself, is seen as tragic in the stories, and since death is always either present or implied, classification of the stories by theme tends to be arbitrary. Classification by technique is even less feasible because it is naturalistic throughout; moreover, any subdivision would reduce the level of literary devices the author uses and not be a true classification at all. Hence the two groups of stories discussed in this chapter may seem to overlap, as indeed they do. The first group, "Stories about Life," does, however, contain stories of lighter tone, with greater use of humor; the second group, "Stories about Death," show actual deaths occurring to the central characters and have a more serious tone.

III *Stories about Life*

Nelly Grissard of "The Robin's House" is a middle-aged widow who has enjoyed love affairs with a Russian, a Greek, and a Chinese.

Nelly has learned her geography, the author waggishly suggests, through her lovers. Her one affair outside her own class was with the artist Nicholas Golwein, a Tartar-Jew, who had just developed a taste for Nelly's favors when she cast him aside for Nord, his Norwegian friend. Piqued, Nicholas produces a plan whereby Nord is to tell Nelly that Nicholas has committed suicide. Nord, amused by the plan, tells Nelly, while Nicholas listens outside her door for her reactions, that Nicholas has hanged himself. While no actual death is present in the story, Barnes uses a trumped-up suicide as the device for triggering the contrast which follows between fat and lively Nelly's appetite for living and Nicholas Golwein's bemusement with the past.

As soon as Nicholas is arranged behind Nelly's door, his mind begins to wander to time past. He feels blissful and allows himself to free-associate at will. Golwein drifts so far away in thought that he does not hear Nord's announcement of Golwein's "suicide," and he scarcely registers Nelly's pained outcries. As his thoughts of Nelly fuse with his ruminations on the past, he assigns a confused godhead to her. She once gave him absolution, he recalls; yet he wistfully admits that even this situation can be reversed, for he forgave her her former lovers. Golwein mixes religion and sex in his musings, but he always moves from the experience of sex to the consideration of religion. As Nelly turns in her conversation with Nord from the supposedly dead Golwein to the living, Golwein turns in his thoughts from the living to the dead. Barnes seems to play upon the traditional figure of the Jew as melancholy, but with comic overtones; for, whether Golwein realizes it or not, he is thoroughly enjoying his sentimentalizing about the past. Golwein is presented as a likeable man and as an accomplished artist; he has a good mind, has traveled, and has had love affairs. His nostalgia for the past, however, overwhelms his positive traits.

The reverse side of bemusement over the past as it contrasts with living for the present is shown when Nicholas, lost in reverie, drops his cane noisily to the floor, rouses himself, and enters Nelly's room to disclose his joke at her expense. When he enters, Nelly, with Nord's shoe in her hand, is kneeling and is apparently about to kiss her lover's foot. Her position may appear to be a trifle ludicrous, but it is, nevertheless, the preferred one: at least, hers is a living foot, and a living act. Golwein's "joke," as he calls it, is less than wholesome; for the predominating influence of the past upon his mind makes this clear. Nelly's final, "Well, go along with you—"

suggests how little Golwein is in her consciousness, now that that episode has ended; for her mind is upon the immediacy of the present experience: the pleasure she anticipates in making love with Nord. When Golwein departs, his own actions and thoughts have reduced him in size from a recent loser in love (and that is still respectable) to the proportions of a small, confused, stereotypical melancholy Jew. Barnes's thesis is that it is better to live, however one lives, than it is to orient oneself to the past, which is always over with and, consequently, beyond reach.

Readers of *Nightwood* will find no connection between Robin Vote and Robin of the title of this story. Nelly calls her home the Robin's House because she is sentimental; and, like so many of Barnes's women, she tends to identify with birds or small animals. Yet Golwein is shown to be far more dominated by sentiment than she; moreover, Nelly, who lives for the present and the future, is sentimental about matters of positive import.

Although some lightness and Barnes's characteristic droll humor appear in "A Boy Asks a Question of a Lady," man's mortality is central in this slight story. The boy of the title, Brandt Wilson, is fourteen and is evidently still innocent about the mysteries of puberty. Brandt's brother, who is two years older, has undergone changes which Brandt cannot understand. When he enters the bedroom of the widely known actress Carmen La Tosca by stepping through her window, he poses his problem, evidently supposing that a famous woman of the world would know the answers. While Carmen lies indolently in bed, the youth stands embarrassed before her. Carmen, who has played both male and female roles on stage, may have a feeling for both forms of sexual identity; but, since she is aware of Brandt's innocence, she tells him nothing that will hurry its loss.

Beneath her civilized appearance is Carmen's knowledge that she is an animal; her wisdom accrues from her use of nature as a basis for her moral and philosophical standards. Life, Carmen can see, is but a short trip from birth to the grave—a bit of time in the sun; and all one can do is enjoy life while one has it. She grasps Brandt's problem at once, telling him that everyone suffers life equally, and not to think of his brother's changes any more. Death, she observes, is the end of everything; and she offers him an adage: "A little evil day by day, that makes everything grow."[1] Carmen administers to Brandt a parting physical touch, emblematic, perhaps, of the wisdom she has imparted to him. Brandt can tell about that touch when he tells the story of how he went to visit the great actress in her bedroom. But Carmen knows, as Brandt will when he is a man, that her touch merely reflected her slight and passing interest in him: her sympathy. Essentially each person must live his life alone.

The title of the story "Aller et Retour" could be translated as "Up and Back," but it implies a journey to and from in French. The words are, in fact, those used by a ticket agent for a round-trip ticket. Barnes's characters do not, however, return exactly to the place from which they departed; but, as in "Aller et Retour," the character is journeying at best, in the direction of his original point of departure. Most of Barnes's important figures are either travelers or have come originally from distant lands; and Madame von Bartmann, who has been separated from her husband, is a Russian who resides in Paris. Her husband having died, Madame is returning to Nice to look after her daughter, Richter. When the story begins, she is at Marseilles waiting for a train to Nice. At Nice she takes a bus to the outskirts of the city. At the end of the story she is departing from Nice in the second-class smoker of a Paris-bound train; but, like a bug traveling a bedspring, she has not returned to where she started.

Madame von Bartmann is presented as a woman whose strength accrues from having learned in her forty years to accept all of life. She registers the foul odors of the streets but does not mind them. She observes a fat woman plucking a robin and filling with feathers the air in which move girls with naked shoulders. The woman's useless cruelty serves to establish the desired tableau: girls and feathers fill the air. The author makes a number of references in this and in succeeding stories to birds, which she relates to women. In this instance, the destiny of Madame's daughter, Richter, seems to be foreshadowed.

Madame, who on the train evinced her common taste by calling out the window for beer, admires in Marseilles the gaudy picture postcards; and she enjoys the smell of tar, the sight of "vulgar" bedspreads in red satin, as well as tin funeral wreaths that are trimmed with beads on wire, that house tin Bleeding Hearts, and that are "beached on a surf of lace."[2] She enters a church where she prays for a "common redemption"—amid images of St. Francis (who called the birds and beasts his brothers) and St. Anthony (who preached sermons to fishes).

At her former home (a mansion on its own grounds) near Nice, she chooses not to enter the house, but strikes out, instead, for the woods behind it. In this environment, surrounded by insects, she meets the daughter she has not seen for seven years. Madame is still holding the key with which she admitted herself through the gate. Her daughter comes "up from a bush" and takes hold of the key. Certainly this odd meeting, essentially feminine in its implications, represents the destiny of women: a gate is to be unlocked, and a birth "from a bush" results.

After the elapse of seven years, the mother and the daughter are ill at ease, although Madame remains good natured; Richter (so named since Herr von Bartmann had hoped for a boy) is timidly respectful; but the two, dissimilar in every way, are virtual strangers. However, Richter now occupies the bedroom that had once been her mother's; and, when Richter announces that she is engaged to marry a Mr. Teal, we learn that she will duplicate her mother's life. Similarly, all humans are repetitions of earlier and later generations; for, as Madame explains to Richter, humans are insects who have invented God, " . . . the light the mortal insect kindled, to turn to, and to die by."[3] They are types of themselves, as in T. S. Eliot's use of this Transcendental motif in *The Waste Land* in which all wars are part of the same war and in which all men are essentially one.

Madame's tragic vision of life's repetitious uselessness is an extension of the author's. Richter weeps once—at the recollection of her dead father. Madame also weeps once—after her attempt with a tangle of truisms to forearm her daughter. Madame's weeping indicates her recognition that nothing can be done; Richter must suffer life even to the pain of death, the tragic payment for having lived at all. Although Richter is a younger dimension of her mother who has learned to be strong, Madame wonders if her wisdom can fortify her daughter. Richter, who is slight, lacks her mother's boisterous health; she is both delicate and timid. Her mother, who has learned that man is "rotten with vice and with virtue,"[4] orders Richter to be morally neutral: to "pray and wallow and cease, but without prejudice." Her final warning is not to "misconceive the value of your passions; it is only seasoning to the whole horror."[5] At this point, Madame understandably weeps; for her tears are a comment on the futility of trying to show her offspring (trying to show anyone!) a shortcut through pain.

Madame is a woman of the world. She plays a huge grand piano with great power (as did Hedvig Volkbein in *Nightwood*, who had three pianos); and, like Hedvig, she likes heavy furniture. Hedvig's furniture has a dark and bloody colored surface, and Madame von Bartmann especially asks about the "black marble Venus." This statue suggests the relationship between passion and death; for this goddess of love, who is carved from the stuff of night, is an emblem of the human predicament. This statue develops the theme of "Aller et Retour" since Richter is bent upon carrying the cycle into another generation: she will marry Gerald Teal, who hopes to have children. Madame is both pained and relieved to hear of the engagement; it frees her of the onerous duties of mother, but at the price of prolonging the cycle of suffering, which is inseparable from life.

Richter will live in a house on the outskirts of Nice; thus, in a sense (since she is already living outside of that city), she will not be one who gets anywhere in her travels. Madame, observing the differences between her daughter and herself, said that she herself grew like a pigeon—a reference to her more robust build and better health. Still, slight or stout, the human race will continue. Madame, having seen her daughter married, departs remarking to herself, "Ah, how unnecessary."[6] Although this remark may seem apropos of nothing at all, the reader understands its significance when he grasps Madame's all-encompassing sense of the arbitrariness of conception in the first place, her cognizance of the enforced suffering which human life is, and her certitude that annihilation is life's final meaning.

Miss Barnes uses the same "frame" for two other stories about life. One of these, "Cassation," is directed at a profound philosophical examination of the nature of "meaning" in life; and the other, "The Grande Malade" concerns social pretensions and transitory value systems. "Cassation," (which means an abrogating, an annulling, or a breaking off) relates the manner in which young Katya chose life with its superficial meanings and rejected a deadly meaninglessness; and the story can be said to prepare the way for "The Grande Malade" in which Katya relates worldly scenes of less profound consequence.

The "frame" in each of these two stories is a Paris cafe, where young Katya tells an unidentified "Madame" her stories. Since the auditress is an American who has just arrived in Paris, she is probably the author herself. "Cassation," Katya's story, was originally titled "A Little Girl Tells a Story to a Lady" when it was printed in *A Night Among the Horses*. "The Grande Malade," originally titled "The Little Girl Continues" when it was published in Ford Madox Ford's *Transatlantic Review*,[7] is about Katya's sister Moydia. Both stories share a light, even indifferent tone that stands in sharp contrast with the emotional response the reader is likely to feel as he reads the two stories.

In "Cassation," Katya's experience began when she went to live with forty-year-old Gaya in her expensive but melancholy Berlin home instead of embarking upon the ballet dancer's career that she had intended for herself. Katya, who was only sixteen when she came to Berlin from Russia, was still quite susceptible to influence; and the test of "meaning" in life began after Katya had lived in the home nearly a year. Gaya has a daughter, Valentine, who was born an idiot. Gaya suddenly announces that Katya must become a companion for Valentine in her timeless, meaningless world. Gaya, an intelligent and strong woman, has hope for the hopeless; an irrational faith that even with Valentine something can be done; and the belief that one should be both ruined and powerful.

But "ruined and powerful"[8] stake out a claim most philosophers would not care to contest. For most philosophies (and religions) aim at a sense of well-being, no matter by what tortured route it is achieved. Existentialism, for all its dark statements concerning the human condition (filled with *angst* and *sorg*), still holds forth the concepts of individual choice and of "Life" (being) as a state to be striven for or (if a person prefers) of "Life" (Being) as an irreducible condition upon which the individual may build. If philosophy cannot hold forth the promise of happiness, it at least seeks to reconcile man to his despair. But Gaya, who actually has turned that despair inside out, has made the ruined state the positive one. For her, the ruined state must become the touchstone of all without herself that is negative or "distancing." The real point of Gaya's Transcendentalism is not in its application to ordinary people; its point and its final test, as well, are in Valentine. Gaya's principle, or religion, builds upon the premise that each person must be like "every one." Her phrase must be understood to include Valentine (Love's Gift), for undeniably she is "one" of the people in the world.

Gaya's timid husband, Ludwig, all but destroyed himself in trying to teach "lessons" to Valentine. Now that Valentine is four and is still making the same buzzing cry—and no other—Gaya applies herself to the task of training her. But where Ludwig would shape Valentine to the world, Gaya is able to see that "man has no destiny"[9] and that there are two ways of looking at the world of objects, people, and events. Ludwig's way is to ascribe *significant* reality to all. It is also possible to take the view (since all things are ultimately doomed to perish), that these same things, people, and events have an *insignificant* reality—that they are *as nothing*. As a result of her views, Gaya instructs Katya in a religion which would create for Valentine a companion in her timeless, placeless, meaningless world. In order for Gaya to do so, she must reverse Ludwig's approach of trying to bring Valentine into coincidence with the world; instead, she must erase the sense of time, thought, people, events, and so reduce the world itself to the Self, so that finally there will be nothing except "only you, only you!"[10]

Katya is unable to accept this regimen for reasons that appear in Gaya's "wild" speech in which she becomes confused as to whether she or Valentine is being addressed. Gaya's words—not to be listened to anyway since to her all things are nothing except for the Self—attempt to create an identification between Valentine and the adoptive sister Katya. This attempt must necessarily be made from outside Katya's Self; this attempt should be made by Gaya, but she cannot impose upon another what is in herself. To postulate that reality is unreal is a subjective possibility only. Since Gaya cannot impose her own subjectivity upon Katya, Katya must leave. When Katya returns for a farewell and finds Gaya "talking" to her daughter by means of the buzzing sounds, she sees that for Gaya the subjective reality has become an actuality. Indeed, Gaya announces that she has found she "can do it [her] self."[11] That she can frame such a statement indicates that she has not lost her mind; she is still able to deal with objective reality (she sends Katya on her way). But she has also laid claim to an understanding that is not understanding—the hope that goes beyond despair. The title "Cassation" and Katya's departure suggest that, for Katya, this subjective interpretation of the nature of reality defines the point beyond which she will not enter another's life.

"The Grande Malade" concerns Katya's younger sister Moydia, who wishes to become "tragique." The sisters are intoxicated with Paris and are determined to "live or die" beautifully. Moydia, fifteen, has taken as her lover Monsieur X, a writer and the protégé of a baron. Moydia, Monsieur X, and Katya hold an all-night drinking party before Moydia leaves for Germany to visit her father. After she leaves, Monsieur X falls ill and is dead in ten days' time. Katya goes at once to the baron and begs of him Monsieur X's cape as a remembrance for Moydia. When Moydia returns from Germany with a high fever, she is put to bed by her sister who shows Moydia the cape and explains how her lover had died. Moydia and her sister begin to drink heavily; Moydia hopes to die; but, when she awakens the next day, she is well. Katya tells "Madame" that Moydia, who always wears the cape she has inherited, is "gay, spoiled, *tragique*. She sugars her tea from far too great a height. And that's all."[12] Now that the sisters know a little French, they plan to move to another country.

Katya's query as to whether the American papers carried anything about Monsieur X's death suggests that the auditress is an American. She is fairly new to France, for she was not there the previous fall when the events narrated occurred; thus she appears to be a persona for the author herself. The sisters are Russian; they have lived in Poland, Holland, and France; but they also intend to live in America. They assume the character of each country they visit. For example, the night of Moydia's party she explains to Monsieur X that Russian women drink to become sober; they are naturally extravagant. She points out that she lets him adore her because "that is the way it is with Polish women." He corrects her, reminding her that she is Russian. Thus Moydia, a Russian-Jew by birth, is in a Polish mood with her lover. Moydia's Jewish strain reinforces her impulse to be "tragique" for to be Jewish in Russia was to be damned.

Forbidden to the Russian-Jew is the champagne which Moydia's grandmother drank on her deathbed and which she insisted that her daughter also drink so that she too would be damned. The dark strain that impels Moydia is explained, therefore, in part by two previous generations, mother and grandmother, of condemned women. Drinking is thematic to the story, for alcohol is used repeatedly as a death ritual and as an antidote to pain. Three nights of heavy drinking occur. When Monsieur X is dying, the baron drinks with him all night so that his protégé can die in an unconscious state. The other two nights, mentioned earlier, are those of Moydia's departure for Germany and of her return therefrom.

"The Grande Malade" is the antithesis of "Cassation," and its title is suggestive of Moydia's romantic attitudes toward both life and death. The illness she seeks to make her "tragique" is essentially a decadent pose, albeit one she sincerely believes in. That the sisters are caught in the superficial ways of the sophisticate is indicated by their attitudes. Katya vastly admires the knee-high boots her father wears and aspires to wear such boots one day herself, and both sisters are entranced by Monsieur X's cape, a kind of trade mark. Moydia announces rather theatrically that she is Marie facing the guillotine, Bloody Mary before the carnage, and Desdemona without Othello. She is all women of notoriety, but she complains that she is "not as bored as they are," and she demands to know when she will become "*properly* bored."[13]

Unfortunately for Monsieur X, the only way he can help matters is by dying, so that through him Moydia can experience loss. Part of the humor as well as sadness of the story is that for one person to become "tragique" another must become a victim. Moydia is the reverse of Gaya in "Cassation" who would cancel all realities and abstract even thought itself into nothingness. To Moydia, the world is very real; and to become a great woman means she must use her mind, her body, and her emotions (which she allows full sway). She cultivates a "throaty voice," just as she begins to sugar her tea from too great a height. Gaya had tried to slip outside of time entirely, but Moydia is immersed in life.

"The Grande Malade" is told in a light, indifferent tone as though nothing of consequence has occurred; and this style, which gives the story its ambiguous quality, was used in "Cassation" to bring the reader to a terrible and harrowing conclusion. In "Cassation," Gaya is the active agent of her purposes; but Moydia of "The Grande Malade" is not. She has no control over Monsieur X's dying, the event that allows her to regard herself as "tragique." Even though a death occurs in this story and not in "Cassation," Monsieur X's death is not made to seem a great loss. The reader feels powerfully the tragic dimensions of the child Valentine's helpless and declining life, but the reader is aware at the end of "The Grande Malade," that life is a very much ongoing affair. The sisters know some French now, and plan to move, presumably, to new adventures; to new dimensions of the Self which remain to be discovered; to new lovers; and to losses of romantically epic proportions.

In "The Rabbit," Rugo Amietiev, an Armenian, leaves his native country and his land to go to New York where he has inherited his uncle's tailoring shop. When he meets the Italian girl, Addie, whom he wishes to marry, Addie declares he is not a hero and insists that he must "do something." The tailor reasons that heroes either rescue people from danger or are great killers—both perilous activities. Rugo thinks either would defeat his intent to win Addie; for, by being either killed or disfigured, he would lose the girl. In the end, he steals a live rabbit from the butcher across the street and strangles it. When Addie arrives, she laughs at his deed; but Rugo presents his killing as an ultimatum: she is to "take it or leave it." Addie becomes frightened and accepts him.

In the *Selected Works* version, a number of changes made in this story which had first appeared in *A Book* sharpen the images, stress the biting irony of "The Rabbit," and strengthen the ending. In the earlier version, Rugo, having killed the rabbit and presented Addie with his ultimatum, steps outside, smiles, and sniffs the air. Addie announces that they are going to get his boots shined. But the later version closes in a more serious mood: Rugo is so moved by his deed that he seems lost and trembling.

The story balances the forces of life—of plowing and planting, on one hand, with killing and death on the other. It balances the clean, healthy life of the farmer against the unhealthy claustrophobic life of the tailor; the fresh country air against the suffocating, gas-fumed air of the city shopkeeper; the mosquitoes of the woods against the human problems of a man called upon to be more than is natural for him. Moreover, the irony in Rugo's life, reveals the monstrous inevitabilities of modern urban man. Rugo, who is content to live the simple life of the farmer in Armenia, has to leave that life to become a tailor (a work he does not like); to lose his cherished freedom; and to toil as though doing penance. He had to do so because he has inherited the tailor shop and because it would not be sensible to continue to live well in the country, when the opportunity has been presented of living very poorly in the city.

As a character, Rugo is the modern man for whom it would be unthinkable not to rise to his highest level of misery. Rugo is the little man who is timid, not bright, and naive. In Addie he has found his urban, female counterpart; for she is cunning and conniving, small and mean. Herself a nonentity, she demands that the man she marry be someone. To deserve her, Rugo must kill since he cannot manufacture the opportunity of rescuing others from danger, since being a savior has a measure of risk, and since Rugo is determined to survive the experience of winning Addie. For these reasons, he selects a rabbit to be his victim. Strangling so puny an adversary as a means of winning one's ladylove might seem the province of a comic story. While the situation does have comic overtones, what Rugo is about is not funny to him. By presenting Rugo's sensitivity, his memories of life-images from his farm days, and his gentleness and by creating a sense that Rugo is being cruelly put on the defensive at every turn by Addie, Barnes shows that, to Rugo, to take any life at all is a monstrous act. Rugo had once loved to stroke his geese which he likened to flowers; killing is not in his nature.

Across the street from Rugo's tailor business is a butcher's shop that runs red with the blood from the day's slaughter. In its showcase are "calves heads in ranks on their slabs, . . . like peeled women. . . "[14] and halved carcasses "showing the keyboard of the spine . . . ."[15] These images not only sharpen the monstrousness of slaughter but evoke, by contrast, Rugo's gentleness. In killing a rabbit, Rugo violates his instincts despite the fact that Rugo eats meat. If it is worth killing a pig for Rugo to have sausage for breakfast, then it should be worth killing a rabbit to win a wife—but the answer must be that it is not. A challenging value system appears because, although we accept the butcher shop as an unpleasant necessity, the rabbit's death seems to violate this bloody need. Rugo's reluctant hands reach through the slabs of the box in what amounts, for him, to an act of murder—a murder in which the rabbit is surrogate for a more dangerous human sacrifice. For Rugo finally has transformed himself from a life-oriented country man to a death-oriented city man. The final irony is that Addie must accept him as having indeed qualified himself for her hand and that Rugo has come to regard Addie and death as the same.

IV *Stories about Death*

In the stories about life, dying has been kept at a respectful distance. We see a pretended suicide in "A Robin's House"; death as the final fulfillment that life inevitably reaches in "A Boy Asks a Question of a Lady"; the ruined life of the child Valentine in "Cassation"; the death of M. X, a minor character deliberately kept well in the background of "The Grande Malade"; and the strangulation of a rabbit as Rugo's substitute for a human victim in "The Rabbit." Barnes also writes stories in which death occurs or is about to occur for her central characters. These stories seem totally unlike the stories about life since they concern such different types of people and life-styles. Nevertheless, the author's underlying philosophical stance remains consistent: life is painful and stupid, even inexcusable; and death is man's sole release from pain and vacuity. These stories contrast life's trials and temptations to the author's concept of death, but death emerges as a positive value in each situation.

Beauty in death is surely the primary quality that "No-Man's-Mare" seeks to convey, for the story presents the naturalist's attitude toward death poetically, through images of natural beauty. In this story, Pauvla Agrippa, the wife and mother who has just died, was young and beautiful; moreover, she wanted to die. Since her baby does not understand that his mother is dead, the infant suffers no loss; and her husband's loss is mitigated by his knowledge that his life will gradually reestablish itself and continue. The story carefully avoids developing the reader's sympathy for Pauvla, for she needed none. The problem for this fishing community (supposedly located at Cape Cod) is to transport Pauvla's body from the promontory on which the village is located to the headlands. Pauvla's sister Tasha reminds the men that the previously uncaptured wild horse known as No-Man's-Mare might be caught and used since it is getting very feeble. The horse is captured, and Pauvla's body tied to its back with fishnet. The funeral procession begins walking along the beach, but after a few steps the horse turns abruptly toward the sea and plunges in it. When a wave washes over the swimming horse, Pauvla's yellow hair can be seen floating behind. When another wave washes over the horse, Pauvla's arms, now freed, appear to be swimming; but the third wave erases both horse and body from sight. Tasha, previously unreconciled to her sister's death, now finds comfort in praying to the sea.

No-Man's-Mare provides the focus of the story. An aging, dying force of nature, her nimbleness in escaping captors and her unwillingness to be touched indicate her natural purity in contrast to which man seems a defilement. The horse is also used as an index to human rapport with nature; for Pauvla has lately approached closely enough to see that the mare has a film over one eye; evidently it is aging rapidly and going blind. Since three children have recently managed to pat the horse, she can be approached as she weakens into death. These approaches establish an implied relationship between the children, the horse, and Pauvla. The children, innocent because of their youth, are still close to nature; but Pauvla, who is not innocent, has a natural quality that approximates innocence: her attitude toward death. For death too is a part of nature, perhaps the only indisputable part; and Pauvla has entered into a deep, almost mystic sympathy with the principle of death. She is fit for the role of the beautiful woman who will be given a unique burial, one that is both poetic and symbolically meaningful; for her burial at sea is emblematic in the story of unending change and of the process of dissolution.

The story reverses the situation used in the one-act play *Kurzy of the Sea* in which a young fisherman catches a mermaid in his net. But the mermaid turns out to be a barmaid and the play a comedy. This story is neither a comedy nor a tragedy, for it so successfully affirms the beauty of death that Pauvla's fate is not made to seem anything but good: it is not even sad. Tasha knows that all things change, that all things decompose, that "the beasts of the jungle are laid low by the insects." Agencies of decay and disintegration, the insects are thus a positive force in the Barnes' inverted naturalism; and Beelzebub, lord of insects, is the true lord of nature. Now that Pauvla is dead, she will become "multiple."

We are reminded by "No-Man's-Mare" of the child's fairy tale with its linear plot and by its tendency to present the bizarre and the monstrous as offhandedly as if they were completely natural. We do not question in a fairy tale the presence of giants, ogres, or mermaids. In "No-Man's-Mare," we read of a funeral procession that is wrested away from men by an aged and dying horse that provides a burial at sea; and such a natural funeral is far more satisfactory than any undertaker could produce. As for the people's success in putting a dead woman's body on a horse that they could never capture until this day, Barnes makes no attempt to justify this coincidence; the action is simply a fact of the story. We have also the child's-tale formula, traditionally magical, in the coming of the third sea wave which obliterates all traces of Pauvla and the mare; and we have reconciliation with nature in Tasha's praying to the sea (after unsuccessfully praying to other things) and of finding comfort "this time".

The title "The Nigger," of Barnes' one story about race relations in the South, calls attention to the disdain many southerners feel for Negroes and thus hints at the theme. Rabb, an aged Negress, is watching John Hardaway, her master, die. Rabb, who had been John's "mammy," shows every concern for her dying master's welfare. John will not have the Negress present when he dies; he will not allow her to eat in his presence, although she has been with him for many hours; but he needs her, and is entirely dependent upon her. Implied during the prolonged dying of John Hardaway is the tenor of a lifetime of interrelationships with the Negro; they were never once conducted on a human equal-to-equal level. The story is characterized by a sense of waiting and by a lurking sensuality which death itself seems to bring into the room.

A contrapuntal effect is achieved between the two characters by a number of means. As John's mind wanders, Rabb crouches in the corner, waiting and watching; when Hardaway is hungry, he calls for broth and Rabb feeds him. Hardaway will not have the Negress eat in his presence because of his "southern gentleman" code; and, when she comes out of the corner to fix herself some soup, he forbids her to eat; yet rather than leave him, Rabb chooses to go hungry. Rabb's soup and Hardaway's broth exist in tentative identification, since food is a necessity and it undercuts the more arbitrary master-servant relationship. Added to this device is the contrast between the powerlessness of Hardaway who is too weak to move and Rabb's crouching posture in the corner. As John nears death, Rabb approaches his bed and ends by standing over him at her full height. Contrapuntally arranged are the white man's hatred and the black woman's sympathy. Rabb herself functions in two distinct ways: just as she is a "good" Negro, solicitous of her master's welfare, so she is also the dark shadow of death crouching in the corner; but, when she is ordered to leave the room, she silently refuses. As she approaches and stands taller and taller by the bedside, so does death more and more closely approach Hardaway; and it ends by towering above him.

The movement of the story is toward Rabb's getting to eat soup in her master's presence; toward the final erectness of the black woman in contrast to the white man's final supineness; toward a consummation of these two disjunct yet interrelated lives. At the moment of death, Rabb leans down to force one last breath of life and death into John's failing body. At this instant, his eyes momentarily open as he expires. Hardaway's final "Ah!" amounts to human consummation at the last possible moment, to a final absolution. The last knowledge Hardaway has of this life is that desperate breath imparted to him by the despised Negro. That one breath vanquishes his entire former life, for implied in it is the racial lie which he has lived and which, even given the opportunity, he could never rightfully live again. Rabb runs her tongue over her lips and raises her eyes; a heightened dignity is now hers. When Rabb gets to eat her soup, we see a final wisdom. Having done all that was to be done, she resumes her own life as it had been before John's illness. The reader admires Rabb; he so despises Hardaway that his death, far from being tragic, seems an improvement.

The theme of Barnes's story "Indian Summer" reminds us of Edgar Allan Poe's view that the death of a beautiful woman was "the most poetical topic in the world," one he used again and again in his poems and tales. Poe sought the creation of beauty, particularly in his verse; but, using the same theme as a "magazinist," he also managed the evocation of considerable Gothic horror in tales like "Ligiea" and "The Fall of the House of Usher." The figure of Madeline Usher throwing her arms around her petrified brother does not inspire us to mourn—nor does Ligiea's return from the grave. Still, the narrators in Poe's poems are properly devastated by their losses.

The same distinction between fiction and poetry is visible in Miss Barnes's dead women. In her poems, the loss is deeply felt; in her fiction and even in *The Antiphon*, we are not invited to mourn. Where death to Poe was a mysterious country whose very borders were in doubt, to Miss Barnes death appears preferable to any condition of life. As the author, Miss Barnes controls the tone of the work; and, if she refuses to mourn, and if the dead character is shown to have preferred death, the reader who feels the loss of life distorts the intention of the story. In "Indian Summer," the death of the beautiful woman occurs but in a social milieu far different from that of "No-Man's-Mare"; and again the author deliberately resists any temptation to see death as tragic.

Madame Boliver of "Indian Summer" has lived an unfulfilled existence for fifty-three years. Plain to the point of ugliness, she has been the tolerated old maid who has lived vicariously through her relatives. Suddenly she bursts into late-blooming beauty; she starts to dress well and to acquire imaginative magazines and rare *objects d'art*. Her home becomes a fashionable salon that attracts students, politicians, and intellectuals. Before this development, she had been ignored; now she finds herself proposed to by men of wealth and position. She accepts a suitor, Petkoff, a thirty-year-old Russian; and she is in the midst of her joyous wedding preparations when she is stricken with illness and subsequently dies. The plot, by any expected human standard, seems tragic; but the story ends not only with Petkoff cursing his misfortune while ludicrously lighting a cigarette at one of the four holy candles surrounding the dead body but with the authorial drollery that in death Madame is more beautiful than ever before. The author's control of the tone throughout the story subverts the reader's ability to extend compassion where it is not sought.

Petkoff is probably the most masculine of Barnes' male characters. Unlike Golwein of "The Robin's House," he is not given to philosophical vaporizings; indeed, he is a man of action, not of words. While he is politely tolerant of his fiancée's talkative acquaintances, he does not feel compelled to join their conversations. Even his entrance into the marital state has been carefully considered; for, as a businessman just getting started in America, he is well aware that falling in love and paying court to a woman cause his own affairs to suffer from neglect. He weighs all considerations carefully before proposing; but, once decided, he sweeps away all competition with ease. A comic figure who takes himself seriously, Petkoff does not fit into a stereotyped characterization; he is drawn too realistically. His lighting a cigarette at one of the holy candles has both serious and comic aspects. He has made a heavy emotional investment and lost, and his "Damn it!" is just selfish enough to remind us that love is more a personal than a shared estate. Petkoff is not thinking so much of Madame Boliver's loss of life as he is of his own of madame. Thus Petkoff embodies in his behavior a truth larger than his own realization but one that expresses the author's view of death.

Madame Boliver, a victim of the conditions that shaped her life, did not ask to be the ugly duckling of her family; she did not request the rare transformation that turned her into a beautiful woman at the age of fifty-three; and she did not choose to fall ill and die. Again, if more pleasantly, in becoming beautiful, she is a victim. And, because the world sees fit to find her in grace, she begins to grow graceful. At the mercy of the determinism of life, she is the passive center both of her life and of the story; but Madame's life ends happily. She has had two years of an adulation she loves at a time when such devotion is, for most women, a receding memory; and her illness only intensifies her lover's attentions. But, despite Madame Boliver's apparently enviable situation, the grave is presented as the preferred destination—even one preferable to the marriage bed. That the story was intended to suggest such a preference is visible in Petkoff's irritated but comic behavior which makes the death difficult to regard as tragic, and in the author's final remark that in death Madame is "more lovely than ever."

In Barnes' two stories with male protagonists, "The Rabbit" and "A Night among the Horses," the men are so manipulated by women that their destinies are shaped by females: Rugo becomes engaged to a girl whom he has begun to consider to be synonymous with death; and John, the hostler of "A Night," is trampled by horses to a death that seems preferable to the life he appeared destined to lead. So long as he cares for horses, John, a rustic who prides himself on his commonness, remains harmoniously intact. Recently, however, Freda Buckler, the mistress of the Buckler estate, has taken an interest in him; she tries to inspire him to rise in the world—to become, for example, a soldier covered with medals. Her behavior is enigmatic, for she seems to retrieve with mockery each new vision of life she gives him; actually, it appears that she really wants him to stop the grooming of horses and become her groom in marriage.

John senses that she is disabling him from the only life he knows and that he would never be happy in her more artificial world of elegance and social contacts. The night chosen as the present of the story is climactic; for, having drunk too much and having indulged in debasing behavior, John rejects Freda and leaves her house. Defiant and confused, he returns to his horses; and he apparently does so to attain the security that he associates with them. Because the horses do not recognize John when he crawls through the stockade enclosure in his evening dress, they trample him to death.

The changes made in this story for the version published in *Selected Works* sharpen the class differences between the hostler and the landowner. John's "frock coat" becomes an "evening dress" and the Buckler "farm" becomes the Buckler "estate". John's feeling that Freda will finally unfit him for both the rustic and social worlds is clarified in the later version in which he sees himself becoming a kind of gargoyle, transformed to the "halt position of the damned" under her influence.

"A Night Among the Horses" deals with two kinds of knowing—natural and social—and with the related themes of betrayal and alienation. John, who had lived in harmony with himself and his horses, betrays his own way of life because of his attraction for Freda. In romantic fiction, we might expect social betrayal to bring about John's destruction; and a normal biological impulse (his attraction to Freda), which collides with social behavior, does influence his fate. John's death is almost retributive: nature, which is represented by a virile stallion, forms the society of which John has been a part. When he has exchanged his hostler's garb for evening dress and when his calm purposefulness is lost because of his confusion over his part in a human social gathering, he is not recognized by the horses and is "cast out" by them.

The reader is not invited to like either Freda or her friends. A small woman with "mousy" hair, she is likened in the later version to a praying mantis, an insect with deplorable social instincts. Her behavior is that of a mechanical toy, and the name "Buckler" may suggest that Freda is encased in some kind of protective armor: her society, her "things," her money. If she reminds us of any of Barnes's other characters, it is the disagreeable Jenny Petherbridge of *Nightwood;* however, Freda is more commanding than Jenny. Freda transfers to John her incertitudes along with her faith in her own value system; and, as a result, John, when he dies, is confused about wanting to rise in *her* world rather than in his own.

Since we think more highly of John than of Freda and since we enter, if only briefly, his mind, he is the central character of the story; and his death becomes the tragic illustration of something. But of what? We do not feel personally threatened by his death: he has been placed in a situation too unique for a universal generalization. If John were to marry Freda, he would be consumed, we are made to feel, just as the female mantis consumes the male after mating. However, John is destroyed by his former association with nature and by natural forces—by the animals with whom he is intimately familiar. In a setting of black night, then, John's death is not so tragic as it at first appears; for his death has been quicker and less painful—certainly less degrading—than the destruction he would have endured at the hands of Freda. Biologically impelled toward woman (who is socially more knowing), man is rendered weak by his inescapable sexual urges that place him at the disposal of the female. Even John's social incertitudes, seen in this light, become his strength; for in renouncing Freda he has chosen, if unwittingly, the nobler and more beautiful death.

John is given a common name and no surname, for his personality is not important to the story. He has no individualized traits, for individuality is not a factor to be considered. The characteristics that are important to achieve the objective of the story are John's rude integrity and strength to say "no" at the critical moment. Having said "no," he finds himself on the outside of society; and all that is left for him is the companionship of beasts. Yet even with them his relationship is tenuous because, although man is an animal, he is not a horse; and he can enter that animal's society only because of its sufferance. In choosing the nobler animal world, John has deliberately alienated himself from a human society that is portrayed as degrading and as one that would surely destroy him. John has not chosen to die; but, given the choices which his life has presented to him, he becomes the victim of a meaningless death somehow preferable to the expectations of his life.

Death, as Walt Whitman observed in "When Lilacs Last in the Dooryard Bloom'd," is indifferent to the dead; they do not suffer. Indeed, as the poet indicated, the dead are rid of the pain and anxiety which constitute life; and they are, therefore, the fortunate ones since only the living mothers, the wives, the sweethearts, and the comrades suffer the loss. Katrina Silverstaff in Barnes's "The Doctors" chooses just such an infliction for her family, for this story concerns a carefully prepared and deliberately executed plan whereby a wife commits adultery and then suicide; and she leaves behind her a bewildered husband and two children. Katrina is a veterinarian; her husband Otto, a gynecologist. In *A Book* (where the story is titled "Katrina Silverstaff"), they first met in a college in Russia; she is Russian and he is a Jew. In the *Selected Works* version, they studied in Freiburg-im-Breisgau, Germany; and, while Otto is Jewish, no mention is made of Katrina's nationality. In the later version, she drops out of gynecology to become a veterinarian; but this change of her profession is not made in the earlier version. As a result of her change of interest, Katrina evinces more interest in animals than in people; but her husband's specialty may suggest his faith in the worthwhileness of the propagation of the human race. Since the couple practices in New York's East Side, they are exemplars of Barnes's uprooted and alienated people.

After ten years of successful practice, two children, and an apparently happy marriage, Katrina abruptly breaks the pattern of her life when the book salesman, Rodkin, appears at her door. She tells him that she is determined to place religion aside and to destroy permanently belief in "some people." In the earlier version, she says that her life is "a lie"; but, in the *Selected Works* version, she says her life is "too arranged." After she has told Rodkin that she will be his mistress, he is admitted to her home on a Sunday; and he departs, the next morning, rather overawed. After he revisits her address and he learns that Katrina is dead, Rodkin takes to drink; he becomes obstreperous in cafés and, finally, seeing the doctor and his two children seated in a café, he laughs and then weeps.

The suicide of Katrina is the central fact of the story. The reader looks for behavioral explanations to find the motive for her suicide: in her career, in her relationship with her children, or with her husband. But Katrina specifically states that she loves Otto and is both pleased with him and proud of him. Neither her children nor her work lend themselves to an explanation either. Katrina is not "depressed" or "despondent." Her motives, we are told, are as mysterious to Otto as the moves in a game of chess. Since Katrina herself must be investigated for the meaning of her actions, her explanation to Rodkin must be accepted as part of a well-conceived plan to commit adultery and then suicide. Her stated purpose is to do something that will make religion impossible to believe in "for a few," and to break her "arranged" life.

For Katrina's family, nothing could ever again make any sense. Her husband and children could not accept any concept of an orderly and just world; for, each time they attempt to reconcile themselves to any scheme of existence, Katrina's senseless suicide could refute the existence of meaningful order. Her final deed constitutes a *geste gratuite* in the manner of Dadaism; hers is an act as meaningless as firing a rifle indiscriminately into a crowded square. However, Katrina bestows upon her family a precious gift—the gift of a matchless reality against which all chimeras of thought have to be tested.

But we do not mean that a mother's highest duty to her family is to commit suicide; indeed, Katrina's motives must be understood to be entirely personal. Any benefit which may accrue to her family is but the by-product of her actions. Her overt, stated motive is to permanently prevent certain people's acceptance of religion. But the conditions that create her plan are not reasoned or rational; they are spontaneous and intuitive. Although she is no older than her husband in years, Katrina is very old in experience; and she lives more rapidly than he. She enters into, accepts, and moves on from each phase of life with an ease of adjustment unknown to most people; and this characteristic explains why she ceased having children. Having experienced motherhood twice she wants no more repetitions. The earlier version in *A Book* hints that ". . . something complicated had entered her mind, and when there are definite complications of the kind that she suffered, there are no more children."[16]

This "something complicated" must be her realization that she is bringing wedded life and death into the world. Hamlet had something of that idea when (outraged or mad) he cried out, as though in fiat, "I say, we will have no more marriages."[17] He was declaiming against the entire process of life and would prohibit it. Nor does the parallel with Katrina end at this point, for Katrina also entertains the notion of doing something "mad." In the *Selected Works*, she makes the point that the will must "attain complete estrangement," but she says in *A Book* that "It takes more than will to attain to madness."[18] The earlier "madness" is thus changed to "estrangement," and this refinement places Katrina's goal within reach of the rational mind. However, the later version argues a deliberate, willed madness; and this status is the point of the story. Katrina has lived "beyond the end" of her life; she has reached a state of awareness in which life itself appears to her as an insanity; she then "wills" her knowledge to her husband and children by her manner of dying.

The story "Spillway" builds upon the paradox that life is most precious to those for whom it is most painful; indeed, the narrative indicates that those who are weakest can be stronger than the apparently strong. A masterpiece of Barnes's art, this story first appeared under the title "Beyond The End" in *A Book*; the title "Spillway" is that of the nine stories collected in the *Selected Works*. Numerous small changes have been made in the later version.

In "Spillway," Julie Anspacher, wife of Paytor Anspacher, has been confined for five years to a tuberculosis sanitarium. Although the doctors have given her no more than six months to live because she has only one lung, and it is damaged, she has somehow survived. Although her case is incurable, Julie returns to her home; and she brings to it a young child named Ann. Ann, Julie tells her husband, is her daughter by a young patient in the hospital who has since died; and the child also has tuberculosis. Having had an affair and a child in secrecy (she had not expected to live long enough for the secret ever to become a problem), Julie is peculiarly distressed: she knows she should feel guilty but she actually does not. She feels, in fact, completed by being a mother; and she thinks that her life, wretched as it has been, has a design which makes sense. Her real objective in returning to her home has been to present herself and her child to Paytor so that he may make her feel guilty.

Sickness has turned Julie's life into a painful struggle with an inevitable death. The child, Ann, although doomed to the same death, is a living extension of herself, and thus goes "beyond the end" of Julie's life; but her sense of guilt is as confused by disease as is her lust. Just as her lust is a product of her fever, so her guilt is a product of vertigo. She has dizzy spells, and has learned to put her head down—to get down on the floor on hands and knees. In so doing, she has the notion that she is abasing herself in contrition for having been untrue to Paytor; but Julie does not feel that she has really been unfaithful since her life is now lived in a hospital. Her sickness has created an enforced alienation from the world at large. Even in normal circumstances, Julie seems to be a direct-speaking person; but her illness has made her impatient and blunt. She has neither time nor breath for extra words, and she has no patience with childishness. Since she has acquired a logical and emotional hardness that is the result of her disease, Julie's sickness, then, is her strength. Her mortality, so imminent, is paradoxically, so powerful that it can destroy her husband. Paytor, for example, rather brags about how easily he makes decisions; Julie, on the other hand, seems dizzily unable to concentrate at all. She is not clear in her own mind as to why she has come home. She has, but rejects, impulses to call upstairs (where the shocked Paytor has retired) as thoughts, fleeting and insubstantial, pass through her mind.

Hours elapse between the time Paytor goes upstairs—presumably to practice on his indoor shooting range and to think about this matter—and the sound of a pistol shot, which may signal his death by his own hand (although we are not actually told that he has killed himself, Julie reacts as if he has). Paytor has been put in the inhuman position of being asked to forgive Julie for having done what for her is only human—and he is called upon to demonstrate a quality of forgiveness he evidently does not possess. Julie Anspacher is a "beautiful" character because she is capable of projecting the kind of stern self-discipline that violates conventional decencies: a discipline that places the character's puny but determined efforts against overwhelming and inevitable forces of destruction.

What makes "Spillway" so interesting is the enforced alienation of character it presents. Many of Barnes's most effective characters are so afflicted, and the best of these are fighters. Victims of circumstance, by birth, by disease, or by some biological oddity, they do what they can, maintaining all the while an amazing fidelity to their own lights.

V *Men and Women*

As we have observed, the focus of Barnes's stories is primarily upon its women characters, for the men usually appear in the background. Some men, like Nord of "The Robin's House" and Petkoff of "Indian Summer," are distinctly masculine by just being the biological "opposites" of women. Others, like John of "A Night" and Rugo of "The Rabbit," are strong enough in their own ways but weak in the hands of the manipulating women they know. Gerald Teal of "Aller et Retour," Ludwig of "Cassation," and Monsieur X of "The Grande Malade" are hardly more than *données* needed for the machinery of the stories.

Barnes's women are depicted naturalistically; but, as they are seen from the outside, little can be gleaned about their thoughts. How they live and how they adjust to their worlds are made clear; what they think is seldom shown. Even in those stories which have to do with the thoughts of their women, a "distance" is invariably maintained. A third-person narrator usually tells the story, sometimes another female character narrates, and the thoughts of the central character are, therefore, secondhand. As a result, the author and the reader are placed "outside" even the central characters. Even if the ideas of Gaya in "Cassation" are exactly as quoted, they are still repeated by Katya to "Madame," who thus stands outside the mind of the character being shown not only with the reader but even with Katya. Perhaps in "Spillway" we enter more fully into Julie Anspacher's thoughts than in the other stories, but her thoughts are shown to be largely determined by her disease, which in its own way is still "outside" although a part of Julie's body.

The stories show that women occupy exactly the same world as men. Whether they are "cared for" by men, as are Richter Teal or Gaya, their lives are distinct; their identities, separate. Julie Anspacher is "cared for" by a hospital, yet the shaping force in her life is her disease, which as surely directs her actions as the smooth skin and handsome body of Moydia directs hers. Life is essentially deterministic, and naturalism predicates that man is an animal caught in his world. Unlike many naturalists, for whom life is a positive if a losing struggle and for whom death is tragic, Miss Barnes regularly presents death in favorable terms and existence itself as tragic.

CHAPTER 3

Three One-act Plays

THAT Miss Barnes ever intended to become a popular playwright any more than she sought to be a popular writer of fiction is doubtful. However, she was likely to be more popular in her plays because, since they are works to be staged, they are open to a far more random audience than are her fictional works. The theatergoer has seldom read the new play to be performed, and he must react to what he sees on the stage against conventions and expectations that are based upon his past experience of the theater. If his expectations are not satisfied, or if the new play seems to ignore the conventions of the stage to which he is accustomed, a failure of communication is likely to occur.

Customarily, the playwright develops his craft with one-act plays (as did Thornton Wilder, Edward Albee, and Tennessee Williams), and then attempts an evening's entertainment: the construction of a full-length play. Miss Barnes's one-act plays were all written early in her career; and her one full-length play, *The Antiphon*, did not appear until nearly forty years later. This long interval alone suggests that Miss Barnes may have chosen a special, selective approach to the theater over a popular one; and *The Antiphon*, which is considered in the final chapter, is undoubtedly her most complex work. Its archaic-to-modern vocabulary, its Elizabethan diction, and its Jacobean plot are fused into a dense, obscure, intricate poetry. The one-act plays, written in relatively straightforward prose, do not pose the linguistic problems of this later drama. Nevertheless, the reviews of her plays, both as published and as performed, consistently characterize these plays as "impenetrable," as "unactable," and even as written in "reprisal" against an innocent audience which the plays defy it to understand.

In the craft of playwriting, there has always existed the problem of developing a metaphor that illustrates the themes underlying the work. In well-written plays, the abstractions are bodied forth in the settings, by the nature of the characters, and through their interactions with their world. In *Hamlet* or in *Oedipus Rex*, the health of the ruler and that of the state are visibly related. All is sterile and barren in Oedipus's Thebes, and the people are "sick" and "unwholesome" in Claudius's Denmark. We witness the eradication of the cancer—a Claudius, an Oedipus—as the plot discloses itself; and we understand their removal to be beneficial to the larger social body. In poorly constructed plays, the thematic material is often imposed upon the visible action: "Take a letter, Miss Jones," becomes an obvious and irksome artifice for injecting thematic material directly into the audience's ears. The playwright, failing to incorporate his themes into the action on the stage, puts his convictions in the mouth of the nearest, likely character even though the words uttered may have little visible connection with the play in progress. Two closely related matters must occur for dramatic communication to work well: first, the playwright must have integrated his thematic material into the structure of the play in the first place; second, the audience must then grasp these issues as the work progresses.

Just at this point Miss Barnes's recalcitrance becomes apparent. As an actress herself in the Provincetown Theatre at the time of her first playwrighting efforts, she knew from the start what had to occur on stage. And as her plays indicate, she is capable of incorporating abstractions into meaningful dramatic forms. What was lacking in her from the start was any spirit of accommodation to the conventions of the theater. She is entirely willing that her plays should communicate something; indeed, they are actually clear and forceful—but only if the audience is capable of recognizing what is being presented. Miss Barnes has brought her highly personal vision (that which Williams reserved for his poetry) to her plays; and that vision must be understood. Moreover, her themes are so well integrated into her plays as to be at once invisible and obvious; for her plots and themes are one. The plays, that is, mean just what they say.

A problem related to that of structure, that is, the successful integration of the theme with the plot line, is found in the nature of Barnes's subject matter. Her plays are about women. Male characters do appear, but they are types who are used as foils to the women characters. Here again, since the reviewers of her plays were themselves male, an unrecognized obstacle appeared. Miss Barnes is an expert at writing about women, but not about women generically; she writes realistically about actual, well-defined individuals. Men characteristically recognize women by their resemblances to females they have known; and, as a result of their own experience, they then tend to categorize them into types. Since the playwright's purpose in each case is to present a fully realized character, her individual traits tend to be taken symbolically rather than realistically by both the critics and the audience.

I Three From the Earth

Miss Barnes's *Three From the Earth* was produced by the Provincetown Players on the same bill with Eugene O'Neill's *The Dreamy Kid* during the 1919–1920 season. Floyd Dell, who regarded the play as "impenetrable," described the audience as "bewildered."[1] To Alexander Woollcott, who was both mystified and enthusiastic, the week's sport was to see the play and try to figure out what it meant. Woollcott, who called the play "inscrutable," confessed that no one understood it—himself, Burns Mantle, Clayton Hamilton—and Woollcott suspected that the author herself had the same problem. He tried unsuccessfully, as he admitted, to relate the play to "the stirring of the masses, and the changing attitudes toward government and capital."[2] He liked the play, however, and expended half a column on an amusing parody of it. He observed that *Three From the Earth* demonstrated how a play can be dramatically absorbing without the audience understanding a word of it.

The play shows three rustic young men who have come to the lavish apartment of Kate Morley, an adventuress, to recover love letters written to her years before by their father who has lately committed suicide. Kate is persuaded to part with the letters, mainly because she is about to be married. John, the youngest of the three, also appropriates a photograph of Kate posed as a Madonna and holding an infant Jesus. An inscription on the back indicates that the baby is also named John, and it also contains "God Bless Him." When Kate tries to bargain for the return of the letters in exchange for the picture, the three refuse. As they depart, John kisses Kate passionately on the mouth, which she protests. James, another brother, retorts, "That's the way you bore him!"[3]

The play is concerned with the unnaturalness of Kate. Some

contrast is established between the tasteful but over-decorated apartment and the garish appearance of the three Carson boys, who in an attempt to dress properly for their visit to Kate, have over-dressed. They wear "super-stunning" ties, russet shoes, and purple asters (which may connote "after-thought" in the symbolism of flowers). Their speech is rude, and Kate berates them for their undeveloped voices. James' reply, "True, we have been shut away from intonations,"[4] is but one of many hints that these young men are not ordinary farm boys. For the Carsons, despite their rusticity, are intelligent, sensitive, and gentle. Kate, in contrast, has to admit to herself that she has a mean streak. Asked how they make their living, John explains "we go down on the earth and find things, tear them up, shaking the dirt off."[5] His phrasing relates to the title and also suggests the boys' elemental relationship to nature.

These young men are able to put their activities into a larger context of significance than that of merely filling the stomach. We understand why, as they proclaim to Kate, they are going to Europe to listen to great men. They have always listened. Their father had brought them up to listen well, to "look stupid," and to say nothing. Their interest in great men and in great thoughts is also attributable to their father's influence, which provokes from Kate a torrential abuse of the dead man. He preferred his wife, a sometime prostitute and not a pretty woman, to Kate, who is handsome. She is critical of the elder Carson for having thought well of himself, for having fathered children, and for his known promiscuity. She exclaims that, for all the boys know, she herself might be the mother of one of them, a remark which prompts John to reply, "So I believe, madam."[6] This exchange forms a rather explicit hint that Kate is indeed John's mother; it occurs early in the play, well before mention of the inscribed photograph.

It seems odd that reviewers should have found the play so mysterious. The audience is apprised of the mother-son relationship in plenty of time to observe meaningfully the interactions of the characters. The three boys are distinctly loyal to one another. Kate is so unnatural as to make no acknowledgement of her son, although she feels free to criticize the manners and appearance of all three. The audience is invited to like the boys and to dislike the shrewish Kate who is going to be married; the Carson boys are going to Europe to hear great men speak. Going to Europe to become wiser becomes, then, the preferred destiny. This play seems to anticipate Miss Barnes's own projected trip to Europe as an interviewer of famous people.

II To The Dogs

Barnes went to the mountains near her own birthplace, Storm-King Mountain, for the setting of *To The Dogs*. The set shows the interior of Helena Hucksteppe's cottage; and like Kate Morley's apartment, Helena's cottage is furnished to reveal an overly exacting taste. The play begins and ends with Helena standing, an arm along the mantle, with her back to the audience.

Vaulting through the window to see her comes Gheid Storm, a well-to-do squire. Gheid has recently lost his wife; and, long an admirer of Helena's beauty, he attempts to pay court to her. He is encouraged by the remembrance that, one night some while ago, Helena had kissed Gheid quite spontaneously. But Helena now gives him very short answers, discouraging his approaches with cryptic epigrams. At the end, Gheid is convinced that he will not have Helena.

This play (which has never been produced), is dramatically effective, if a bit "talky," because its characters and their actions become dramatic metaphors for its theme. That Helena begins and ends the play with her back "almost squarely" to the audience is an apt symbol for her type: a private woman, she has "turned her back" to the public world. Helena is not a hermit but a recluse. When she returns to the city each fall, she no doubt selects there the areas and the individuals with which she is willing to concern herself. Moreover, a number of rumors Gheid has heard hint of a rather active sex life; because of these tales (which Helena does not deny), we may assume that Helena does not live entirely alone, even at her cottage; but she nonetheless lives a private life. Helena is both an individual and a self-sufficient woman. Her costume and appearance underscore the "singular sadness" of her body. The phrase may suggest a double meaning: Helena is perhaps fated by nature to remain single but to remain single is unnatural, hence sad.

Helena imparts—in her body, in her hair, in her dress—a sense of the woman who knows a great deal. On the other hand, Gheid reveals in his expressionless face an essential naiveté. Gheid, "well brought up," has learned to be a caretaker of the world he inherited;

but he has yet to examine that world. Although a widower with a young son, life has taught him nothing. Moreover, as Helena points out, he has yet to make a start for himself.

The drama which follows illustrates the profound distance between knowledge and innocence. Gheid approaches Helena in anger and is rebuffed by her passivity; he kisses her impetuously and is rebuffed by her indifference. When she actively invites him to touch her, he does not know how. Helena makes clear to Gheid that she can be touched but only by her own kind. Although Gheid is capable in the public world of being the country squire, he is still a child in the private world of affectional relationships.

Helena speaks of her life as a kind of death, of her passions as a form of decay. Gheid, she says, may one day come to possess a woman like herself; but that could occur only after he has known a great many women, and after a number of years have passed, by which time she would be an old woman. The imagery of the play supports Helena's attitudes, for it is autumnal; the leaves are turning color. Helena is a woman of the fall season, emotionally and psychologically; Gheid, who tends his lawns without enjoying the task, is in the summer condition.

Part of Gheid's pride and his self-respect is to be able to tell Helena that he has a "clean heart" and that he has "never gone to the dogs" for the sake of love. But such remarks, far from recommending him, arouse Helena's anger since they actually signal his disqualification. To Helena, love and wisdom are related but not in ordinary ways. She speaks of herself as being objective and unemotional. She has spent her "whole life in being [her] self."[7] She is thus unwilling to hear Gheid's proposals because she is fully occupied. In Helena, the reader is presented with a woman who defies ordinary understanding. The rumors concerning Helena would have it that each spring she drives a different man to her cottage at the end of a whip. But the reader has no way of confirming the rumors. Helena is, in a sense, an early cousin to Miranda of *The Antiphon*, who also is sexually experienced, wise, self-reliant, single, and unwilling to reveal any of her nature.

III The Dove

The Dove was produced by Samuel Eliot of Smith College at the Studio Theatre in 1926. The setting, a long and low New York apartment, has a shape similar to the apartment of Kate Morley in

"Three From the Earth," which the Carson boys described as a woman's room. Garishly done in pinks and reds, and furnished with many guns and swords, it is intended to be "luxuriously sensual." As with Kate's and Helena's decorating, the Burgson sisters have over-done it.

Three female characters—the two Burgson sisters, Amelia and Vera, and a young girl of about twenty known as the Dove—appear in this comedy. At the play's start, the Dove is polishing a large sword while she awaits Amelia's return. It soon becomes clear that the sisters are on their way to becoming old maids. They have dirty minds and a longing to be "perverse," but they have in fact done nothing but look at pictures of courtesans and bathing girls, read a few French novels, and kept some pets whose mating habits they avidly observe. They have, in other words, sublimated their libidinal drives into voyeurism.

The Dove deals with the related themes of loneliness, inhibition, and obscenity. The play protests against the restrictions people impose upon themselves which cause them to substitute second-hand gratifications for actually living their lives. The use of arms in the properties makes possible a *double entendre;* for to be held in human arms is the desired consummation; and Vera's waking dream reveals this much. She sees herself as a china doll whose head and arms are broken but whose china skirt then becomes soft and flexible. Hands and heads prevent this, and a skirt becomes as stiff as Dresden. Vera has worried that she and her sister will never become "perverse," but the play argues that actually the reverse is the case. In getting their lives out of pictures and books, the sisters are already perverse; if they would but live their lives, either lesbian or heterosexual, they would cease to live as they do.

The Dove, a slight, red-haired girl, seems young and innocent, yet her speech is very knowing. The Dove met both Vera and Amelia at the same high fence in a park. She bowed to Amelia when they met "in an almost military fashion, [her] heels close together. . . ."[8] In this fashion the Dove presents her own image of herself as a boy-girl who has a penchant for the stiffness of military bearing. The high fence by which she met both sisters is the one separating the invert from "straight" or heterosexual people.

Vera's dream implies frigidity and seems to confirm her later remark that the bones seem willing to express themselves but the flesh is not. The Dove points out that the reverse may be the case:

the flesh is willing, but the bones resist. In either case, the action of the play until Amelia's entrance develops a sense of Vera's impatient waiting and of the Dove's watchful waiting. Vera is waiting for her life to begin, but she has no way of making that happen. The Dove is waiting for the moment when she can assume her own true role as the lover of the two sisters.

The Dove's position is existential (although the term itself would not be coined for another decade), in her insistence upon free will—choice—in the presence of apparent deterministic necessity. She is "impatient of necessary continuity. . . . [She wants] the beautiful thing to be, how can logic have anything to do with it, or probable sequence?"[9] We see here an anti-deterministic stance; the premium is placed upon taking one's life boldly in one's hands and making of it what one wants. No wonder, then, that Vera is afraid of the Dove; for the latter's name is misleading. Despite the Dove's white gown, her well-kept hair, and her slight figure, she is a bold and advanced thinker; and she subscribes to a kind of existential commitment: a thought is but an empty gesture until it is transformed into an act. She even challenges the apparently iron logic of "continuity."

Animal imagery abounds in the play, as do images of decay. The Dove stated that she is fond of moles (for their underground affiliations), and she has recently been offered some dancing mice. Like the animals, the Dove refuses to have a past; she wishes, indeed, that everyone could escape having a "biography." To such personal questions as has she had lovers, her characteristic reply is "Who knows?"

Amelia is the dominant of the two sisters, and the Dove confesses to a love for her. If the Dove can win Amelia, she has won both sisters. Hence the climax of the play begins to shape itself upon Amelia's entrance. Although she keeps telling herself that she is in excellent humor, Amelia is actually frustrated and miserable. She complains of the tedium of having to maintain her figure; she wants to tear all the wires out of the house, destroy the city's tunnels, and "leave nothing underground or hidden or useful. . . ."[10] She has by this time worked herself into a passion of despair, and she ends by falling to her knees before the Dove. The language she uses in the climactic moment of her despair is implicitly sexual: "Give me the sword! It has been sharpened long enough, give it to me, give it to me!"[11] Amelia blindly reaches for the sword, but her searching hands find instead the Dove's hand, which she seizes. The Dove then "bares Amelia's left shoulder and breast . . . and sets her teeth in."[12] Amelia stifles a cry. The Dove rises, pistol in hand: bows; and goes into the entranceway. When a shot is heard, Amelia rushes out to see what has happened. She returns holding the painting *Venetian Courtesans* which has a bullet hole drilled through it, and announces, "*This* is obscene!"[13]

While watching this puzzling, cryptic, symbolic play, the audience (it can be assumed) would be in a complete daze when this scene occurs. For all they know, the Dove may have shot herself. Amelia's exclamation. "*This* is obscene!" when she reappears with the punctured painting puts a wry but happy ending to the play. The italicized "*This*" suggests that Amelia now realizes that the Dove, by shooting the picture has erased obscenity from the sisters' lives, for she will replace it with something real: her love, for which they have unwittingly yearned. Amelia's capitulation empowers the Dove to act, to become the "male" figure in their household. The effect upon the audience of "*This* is obscene!" would probably be comic; for the audience might well take it as a comment about the play, about shooting holes in paintings, or about lesbianism. But, in fact, this comment is fitting because of the play's theme: it is better to live—whatever the manner—than it is to dream about living. A well-written comedy, *The Dove* would be certain both to mystify audiences and to give them some uneasiness. In its symbolism, its overtly sexual dimensions, the play is "outrageous" in the better sense of the word.

The Dove is not an early Robin Vote, *Nightwood's* alluring central character. Robin is physically boyish where the Dove is slight. The Dove's hair is elaborately done; Robin's hangs down like a mane. The Dove is fully conscious and aware, but Robin moves in a dream, her feet finding their own way. The Dove, while not talkative, is articulate; but Robin seldom speaks at all. Robin is unable to be interested in anyone but herself, while the Dove is much more outward-looking. The Dove is aware of causality and of the determinism of things; and she *wills* a life for herself which establishes its own reality in defiance of accepted models. Robin does not reason. The Dove is experienced and would forget; Robin's experiences leave nothing behind, hence she remains innocent. The Dove, consciously waiting, knows exactly what is going to happen; Robin, scarcely conscious at all, is hopelessly lost. Both share the boy-girl biological strain, and both prefer actions to words.

Miss Barnes's plays are well written, and her plot and characters *are* the message. Symbolism is present, but incidental, for the theme and story are fully integrated. Reviewer and audience confusion may well have been caused by "looking for meanings" rather than by observing the play itself. Again, that insistence upon her own personal vision that is so characteristic of Barnes probably created a too great distance between what the audience expected (by way of the "conventions" of theater) and the realities it was being called upon to recognize.

CHAPTER 4

Ryder

IN *Being Geniuses Together*, Robert McAlmon emphasized that the expatriated writers of the 1920s who regarded Paris as their headquarters were both immensely active and immensely creative. It had become fashionable in the United States to look upon this group as being "lost" in some cataclysmic way. The term, originating in a remark by Gertrude Stein, was to the effect that the young writers in whom she interested herself were part of a "Lost Generation."[1] Yet this same group of writers—active, creative, busily experimenting with their craft—included such names as Ernest Hemingway, Djuna Barnes, William Carlos Williams (briefly), Edith Sitwell, James Joyce, McAlmon, Ford Madox Ford, Ezra Pound, Mina Loy, John Dos Passos, and a number of others.

For this group, the impact of World War I had loosened the ties and soured the hopes of an entire generation of writers. Hemingway employed the "Lost Generation" thesis in *The Sun Also Rises* when he had Bill Gorton describe to Jake Barnes the stateside response to this expatriated group. Barnes, an American newspaperman living in Paris, was to Bill Gorton an expatriate: "You're an expatriate. You've lost touch with the soil. You get precious. Fake European standards have ruined you. You drink yourself to death. You become obsessed by sex. You spend all your time talking, not working. You are an expatriate, see? You hang around cafés."[2] Bill Gorton was having fun with Jake Barnes, but he echoed the resentments and suspicions of the times.

Robert McAlmon was impatient with this kind of criticism and even of the supposition that the "lost" generation was that uniquely "lost." He readily disposed of the accusation that expatriates drank too freely by observing that the scouts who returned to the States with intelligence about the Paris crowd were equally thirsty. As publisher of Contact Editions, as a literary man, and a *bon vivant*,

McAlmon knew a great many writers and was quick to praise their industry. Miss Barnes, a close friend in those years, was one of his best examples: ". . . Djuna Barnes worked with . . . zeal when writing *Ryder* and the *Ladies Almanack* for which she did drawings. She coloured the drawings in forty copies of the book by hand. Ford [Madox Ford] and Joyce and Morris Werner were all working steadily too, but not with the near-fanatical devotion to labour with which Djuna and Mina [Loy] toiled."[3] McAlmon was equally impatient with the "Lost Generation" label which had been so easily applied to those writers: ". . . Josephine Herbst, was working on a trilogy of American life, which is one of the surer signs that American writing is growing up and healthily, disregarding that assinine "lost-generation" attitude. We are all lost generations until we know we are lost and then there is a chance of salvation."[4]

The 1920s produced many experimental works, some of which proved evanescent (like the instant art of Dadaism) while others became landmarks in literature, as well as signposts studied by subsequent writers for their own direction. Hemingway's achievements in language influenced a whole school of imitators. As for Joyce's *Ulysses,* the stream-of-consciousness technique has been so widely imitated that the adjective "Joycean" is now readily understood. Eliot's *The Waste Land,* which looked both backward and forward historically and culturally, has influenced the writing and challenged the thinking of nearly every modern poet. Ezra Pound, too, helped to shape the reading of, and experimentation with, Chinese and, later, classical, mediaeval, and Renaissance forms. In 1928, Djuna Barnes published two works—*Ryder* and *Ladies Almanack*—both experimental in form and style, that were to abrogate her earlier commitment to the more conventional narrative techniques of *A Book* and thus free her for the truly creative, stylistic achievements of *Nightwood* and *The Antiphon.*

Ryder, published in 1928 in New York by Horace Liveright, was followed, three months later, by the appearance of *Ladies Almanack,* privately printed in France. McAlmon took credit for making the printing arrangements for *Ladies Almanack* with Darantière of Dijon, the printer of the first edition of *Ulysses* and for Contact; and Barnes' work was published anonymously by "A Lady of Fashion." Actually fifty copies, not forty as McAlmon has said, were hand-colored by the author; the first ten were signed; the remaining forty, colored but not signed. The edition ran to 1,050 copies.

Although *Ryder* and *Ladies Almanack* appear to be stylistically related, they are not really alike. *Ryder* is a compendium of styles ranging from the Bible to nineteenth-century Sentimentalism, while *Ladies Almanack* maintains a consistent eighteenth-century language of Manners, complete even to the use of capitalized nouns, "humor" names, and the high-comedy devices of wit. Moreover, the source material and the plots generated therefrom are completely different.

I *Plot and Theme*

For her characters, themes, and perhaps to a certain extent, plot, Miss Barnes turned in *Ryder* to her own childhood years when she was growing up on the family's Long Island farm. Written as a picaresque mock-epic, the novel employs a number of styles in prose and poetry which parody their antecedents; but each style consistently recurs. Usually a given style is associated with a particular character, as for example, the mock-Chaucerian verse that is used to describe Dan Wendell. In *Ryder*, plot and theme are at times advanced simultaneously but, at other instances, separated; thus in certain chapters we can see no connection at all with the plot, for the theme is being dealt with in the form of a parable or of a poem that is only abstractly connected with the total work. Thus *Ryder* is organically and artistically whole and thematically unified, while at times it appears mystifyingly incoherent to readers looking for a solidly linked plot-theme construct.

The plot of *Ryder* concerns a rural family in which Wendell Ryder, the title figure, has fathered two families—one with his legal wife; the other with his mistress. Both women, their eight children, Ryder, and Ryder's mother share one house. The novel's first twenty-nine chapters provide a sketch of the origins of the family, the development of Wendell's philosophy, and his way of life. These chapters detail, with the low-comedy devices of situation and action and with the high-comedy devices of wit, typical family events such as when the two women quarrel and make up or the children advance their claims for attention. With chapter thirty, "The Cat Comes Out of the Well," the theme, hitherto unstated, is abruptly projected to the fore and remains clearly in view until the novel's conclusion. This theme shows a developing conflict between social "propriety" and Wendell's unorthodox life style. The reader has been so variously entertained until this time as to forget, perhaps, that another real world exists: the one usually referred to as "society." Ryder's independent life-style is gradually encroached upon in the last twenty-one chapters by social forces which threaten to destroy his family. He is asked to account for not sending his children to school, even though they are being given perhaps a superior education at home. He weathers this storm only to be confronted with the charge that he is living immorally with two women. When he is given the ultimatum to purify his life-style or to be prosecuted by the law, Wendell is placed in the position of having to choose between his two families; and the novel closes with his discovery that he cannot make a choice.

II *Characters*

The first chapter, "Jesus Mundane," is the annunciation of Wendell Ryder as mock-savior. Unlike Jesus, who could save others but not himself, Ryder can save no one. Using a King James biblical diction, the godlike author "creates" Ryder as a limited man who cannot understand his own life. Above all, he is warned against "fanatics," for the religionists will be his greatest threat. Ryder's unorthodox views put him in opposition to the code of the Puritans, for the American turn-of-the-century society is monogamous and believes in the grace of the work-ethic. It trusts unquestioningly its institutions; marriage, the public school, and the social worker are its means to happiness and order. Ryder cuts against this grain in every way; for, a hedonist, he preaches the virtues of polygamy; he sedulously avoids work, especially work done for other men; and he regards public school education as both inadequate and corrupt. Naive, thoughtless (although he is a man of ideas), and promiscuous, Ryder regards himself as destined to impregnate women; hence he is the Father, in a waggish reversal on Christian symbolism.

Living with Wendell Ryder is his legal wife, Amelia, and Kate Careless, his lifelong mistress. With Amelia he has had five children; with Kate, four, but one of them dies shortly after birth. Wendell's aging mother, Sophia, is also part of the household. Since Wendell only works his farm enough to supply food to his family, and has no other income, Sophia, now aged seventy, has been secretly writing begging letters to wealthy men from her past life. Wendell's only attempt at working for hire, his three weeks as a drug store clerk, was a dismal failure; therefore, Sophia's successful appeals for money enable the large family to live in some comfort.

A kind of biblical logic (in the "who begat whom" form) organizes the early chapters. In chapter 2, "Those Twain—Sophia's Parents!"

Wendell's maternal grandparents are sketched. Aging Jonathan Buxton Ryder "eased himself in his trapdoor trousers with pride"[5] while his wife, Cynthia, is delivered of her fourteenth child. Cynthia's mind has wandered a bit in late years, but she has sense enough to see that Sophia, her oldest child, is pregnant. Sensing death at hand, Cynthia charges Sophia to nurture her own baby at one breast; Sophia's at the other.

Sophia had gone to Latin tutor John Peel for her lesson and had come away impregnated. Three days after giving birth to Wendell, Sophia married her tutor; but, taking an early dislike to Peel, she gave her son the Ryder name. Like Nora in *Nightwood,* Sophia kept a salon. Sophia, like Nora, is a mother figure; but, where Nora never gave birth, Sophia is thrice a mother. Sophia disarms the wives of men she likes by asking them to call her "Mother." Older women are flattered, and the younger ones are mollified. By the age of forty, Sophia had traveled all over Europe. Her pictures are an archeological history of her interests, for she pins new ones over the old until they are two inches thick on the walls. A gentle rap at her door by Wendell inspires her homemade pen, loaded with soot-ink, to raptures of epistolary despair. "My dear, dear, do not fail me now, my son's eyes cry vengeance upon me for that he suffers in that mould of too great measure of genius in which I cast him . . . . "[6] Dressed in immaculate linens, Sophia casts about her an outer garment of rags to receive her alms. She is "beggar at the gates, to be queen at home."[7]

The fourth chapter, "Wendell is Born," brings the main character into the world on page twenty, a considerable advance over the leisurely pace of Laurence Sterne in *Tristam Shandy.* As a child, Wendell received instruction from a beggar on stilts who looked in his window one day. When the stilt walker observed that he made a great arch and that greatness is always so commemorated, his wisdom is not lost on Wendell. In a later chapter, he creates with his own nakedness an arch for his women to look up to when he stands astride the upstairs trapdoor, laughs down at them, and observes that they are seeing their "destiny." Wendell is Jesus Mundane: he was begot, his mother insists, not by John Peel but by a dream of Beethoven. The great composer, she explains, passed through her, boots and all, without so much as an apology. She assures Wendell that, since he was created not by cohabitation but by an "infusion," he was immaculately conceived.

Five fallen maidens lying amid branchless trees topped with

foliage grace chapter five, "Rape and Repining!" The author's drawing shows girls in Puritan costume lying tumbled, their pantaloon petticoats peeping beneath long dresses. The girls, who have expressionless faces, are evidently asleep; but their arms which are outspread betray some recent activity in which (though they keep their feet tightly together) they have evidently been vanquished. They lie amid polelike trees while overhead storm clouds gather.

The richness of this chapter cannot be paraphrased. It is thick with mock-sympathy and hilarious with irony. The burden of its statement is that girls fall prey to the sexual desires of boys; that once fallen, there can be no recovery of innocence; that the world casts heavy opprobrium on those who fall; that falling must be; that fornication leads to undesirable consequences; and that, although nature is irresistible, to give birth is to extend the reign of death by another generation. While the text is against fornication, the chapter's theme is visibly a celebration of sexual activity. Immense vitality infuses the lines: "What ho! Spring again! Rape again, and the Cock not yet at his Crowing! Fie, alack! 'Tis rape, yea, Rape it is and the Hay-shock left a-leaning! Ah, dilly, dilly, dilly, hath Tittencote [the county seat in England where Wendell wooed Amelia] brought forth a Girl once again, no longer what she should be, but forever and forever of To-morrow and yet another day!"[8] And mock-despair wails at the loss of virginity: "A Girl is gone! A Girl is lost! A simple Rustic Maiden but Yesterday swung upon the Pasture Gate, with Knowledge nowhere, yet is now, to-day, no better than her Mother, and her Mother's Mother before her! Soiled! Despoiled! Handled! Mauled! Rumpled! Rummaged! Ransacked! No purer than Fish in Sea, no sweeter than Bird on Wing, no better than Beasts of Earth!"[9] The author, in high dudgeon, scolds with increasingly severe invective all girls who are brought to earth. Such girls are wasting time, violating morality, and mixing the order of the generations. This delightful chapter, rich in its parodies of eighteenth-century prose, ends gently enough with a reminder of spring: "It is Girls' Weather, and Boys' Luck!"[10]

Juxtaposition is used in "Rape and Repining!" to advance the theme while the plot is temporarily suspended. This chapter, which is sandwiched between the previous "Wendell is Born" and the following "Portrait of Amelia's Beginning," amplifies the theme that Wendell's wooing, marrying, and begetting with Amelia constitute but one aspect of a great and general principle of life. Neither Wendell nor any other character is specifically mentioned, yet

"Rape and Repining!" generalizes about conditions that bring men into the world and artistically unites Wendell in his beginnings with Amelia in hers.

In chapter 6, Amelia de Grier, one of twelve children of Hugenot stock, is introduced at age seven (in 1869) amid a flurry of chicken feathers. Having caused consternation in the henyard, Amelia was chased about by her father, John Johannes, with a horsewhip. The following day, the whip at his side, John died in his bed; and it is made clear that before his death he had been the right father to prepare Amelia for Wendell.

After Amelia was orphaned by her mother's death, she took her share of a small inheritance to London, to study music. She practiced voice and violin until she met Sophia and Wendell. Sophia "adopted" Amelia with her characteristic "call me Mother." The upshot of this new relationship was that Amelia gave her legacy to Sophia, abandoned her studies, and moved in with the Ryders. Sophia heard the story of Beethoven from Amelia, which she promptly plagiarized into her own immaculate conception of Wendell, which is described in "How Wendell Was Conceived."

The eighth chapter, "Pro and Con, or the Sisters Louise," serves as the obverse of "Rape and Repining!" Again, juxtaposition advances the theme at the expense of plot. Two young lady pianists, twin sisters each named Louise, serve as a chorus to the affairs of Wendell. The sisters appear only in this one chapter; and, unless their purpose is grasped, "Pro and Con" seems to fragment the novel. The indistinguishable sisters share hooked noses and a home, conversations, and the piano keyboard. While they play duets, they converse; and the nature and the language of their talks evoke Restoration comedy of Manners dialogue. The twins are titillated by news of Wendell and enjoy a bit of juicy gossip. Wendell has made certain advances, declaring to both sisters that, until they have been in bed with him, they have not experienced satisfaction. As one sister puts it, "He maintains . . . that no woman, however fanciful, however given to speculation and to trial, to coquetry and to gorging, can be happy without his peculiar kind of collusion."[11]

Open-minded as the sisters are, they can only see advantage for Wendell in his proposal. They are aware that Wendell has been "carrying on," simultaneously, with six women of assorted ages. The spinsters offer an alternative to Wendell's aggressions. In *Ryder*, the author characteristically defends her characters, their doings, even their names. Here for example, the sisters who refuse Wendell, create a contrast between a life of apparent gentility (playing Brahms duets, stitching fancy embroidery, the vicarious pleasures of sexual gossip) and the actual indulgences of six lusty women. "Pro and Con," having presented both ways of life, leaves the reader to decide which life is preferable; hopefully, his decision will be in favor of deeds and not of words.

In chapter 9, "Tears, Idle Tears!" Amelia has an impassioned but futile conversation with her sister Ann on the night before Amelia sails for America. The response of Ann, who functions like the twins of the previous chapter, indicates the motives and responses of the spinster. Ann's mouth is filled with platitudes: "You can be sure of nothing but death and rent-day, and it never rains but it pours, and it were better never to have been born."[12] But Ann's wagging tongue slips into "A place for everything and everything in its place,"[13] which causes her to imagine a rolling ship as a place in which people get tossed topsy-turvy. She advises Amelia to be safe, by marrying Wendell before sailing.

The sisters, ever incompatible, represent opposite sides of the feminine response to sexuality. Ann has had ten offers of marriage, has jilted three suitors, and will not marry a man she cannot respect. Since no such man exists, she will not marry; she goes into service to support herself. Interspersed through the rest of the novel are epistolary chapters that reveal the sisters' correspondence, and these chapters serve to relate the domestic vagaries that Wendell perpetrates to the equally bizarre events of the larger world.

Amelia, "deep in the slough of love,"[14] is as blind as Ann to the truth about men but in a reverse fashion. Amelia is convinced that, despite Wendell's opposition to monogamy, he is faithful to her; Ann retorts that men are incapable of recognizing their own beds. She believes that Wendell's free thinking will inevitably lead him to the manure heap of life, but Amelia is equally certain that it will lead him to her own Church of England. In defense of her future mother-in-law, Amelia repeats the story of Wendell's immaculate conception by Beethoven; and she apparently fails to recognize that she was herself the source of the original story. To Ann, the tale proves Wendell to have been a bastard, for "Does she not as good as put it to you that she got him running about on an intransitive verb . . . ?"[15] The sisters weep in each other's arms when they part; Ann is convinced that the American Indians will cut off Amelia's ear and mail it back to her.

In chapter 10, which imitates the *Canterbury Tales,* we find parodic Middle English couplets and even the arrangement of some rhymes in the style of Chaucer. Under the title "The Tale," the hero is called Dan Wendell, which the author's convenient glossary translates as "Wendell the Philosopher." Wendell is seen lying abed and thinking while his wife sleeps, and Kate Careless dreams of ways "for the swerving of that tool" in her direction. Known as "Wonder" and "Hendy" (handsome), Dan Wendell's midnight thoughts are also of its proper use. He envisions having as many children as there are pieces on a chessboard. Even more tempting is the thought of having a deck of children—fifty-two in number—and perhaps a joker as well.

Dan Wendell studies a method for making bread from bran, so he can feed both children and cattle from the same bin. He sees no essential difference between children and cattle nor, for that matter, between women and cattle. In one fell act he had pierced the ears of the one and the noses of the other. Dan Wendell saves the sacking from hams to make shirts and diapers, but this act appears to be the limit of his economic thrift. In a desperate physical economy, he fashioned for use on Kate "an oxen bone/ That with pleasure might his Kate groan."[16] But, after one trial, Kate refused to have anything to do with Wendell's makeshift substitute.

Wendell as cosmic man, the representative of all men, advertises in "Cattle Call" that for two dollars he will salve all sores, solve all problems, and cleanse all sinners; for he is

> Adviser, father, brother, friend in ruth;
> The one and only vat of seething truth
> Wherein the garment of repentance, flung,
> Returnes twice as light and neatly hung . . . [17]

Wendell interests himself in travel (but only in books); and he exhausts himself, imaginatively, by climbing high peaks. He turns to the gospel of polygamy and, books in hand, carries his crusade to astonished neighboring farmers.

Perhaps the depths of Wendell's philosophy is reached when he questions the presumed differences between animal and man. Has he not seen the love-light in the eyes of weasels and lynxes? Does not the same "hammer" beat within the breast of Hisodalgus, his horse, and his own? Eventually, Wendell puts his thinking to the test. Since flattery of one's ancestors seems the strongest inspiration to cause others to speak, he addresses all his animals at once, telling them they are all wellborn. Man, he tells them, is unwilling to cut the throats of those who can reply; and he thus motivates his animals to articulation. He exhorts them to eat and pass a favorite herb each day, the odor of which will rise to heaven in divine complaint.

A miracle of sorts does occur. The animals all turn soft eyes upon Wendell; and, when Hisodalgus rears and places his forelegs on Wendell's shoulders, he looks long and deeply into his master's eyes. Wendell's attempts at communication produce indecisive results; although he is related to the animal world, man is nonetheless alienated from it by the consciousness of his mind.

A catechetical style is used in chapter 17, "What Kate Was Not." Through the raising and answering of a series of questions, a justification of the character of Kate Careless is established. Other names suggest a Kate who would not be able to fill the role demanded for her. She might, for example, have been "Kate Why-Not," a rather laconic type or "Kate-The-Doll," a symbol of virginity to the nation. Through a series of incarnations, she might start as "Kate-Cast-Pot" (the girl who empties her chamber pot out the window upon the head of a venerable judge); appear as a fish-vendor; and finally die as "Kate-The-Swoon," of a fallopian pregnancy. In order to correct this fate, she would have to become "Kate Careful," an impossibility. Hence, as a result of possibilities rejected, Kate Careless emerges as the best name.

Chapter 17 forms an apology for Kate, and chapter eighteen, "Yet for Vindication of Wendell," defends Wendell by advancing in Chaucerian couplets the value of his being a stud for women. Wendell's service to women is holy, since procreation is life's sole meaning. Even a queen can be destroyed by unfulfilled passion. Other lonely women include Elaine who drifts through all time in her shallop; Helen, whose face was timeless; and Leda, "caste" to the swans. Even the nun, chained by invisible links of prayers, is thus neglected by God who omitted from His creation consideration of the woman's passionate nature. Thus Wendell is "shoped" to satisfy their ends.

In chapter 19, "Amelia and Kate Taken to Bed," Amelia bemoans childbirth and cautions her daugher Julie never to let a man touch her. At the same hour, Kate is in labor; and her condition causes Amelia to realize that a night nine months before Wendell had not really gone, as he said, just for firewood. Although Wendell declares himself competent to deliver his own children, Julie sends her brother for Dr. O'Connor who arrives on "doctor's feet," and who calls for scissors and silk twine, and who is essentially the same Matthew O'Connor who becomes the major spokesman of *Nightwood.* Amelia is delivered of a son; Kate, of a daughter.

The biblical language of chapter 21, "Wendell Dresses His Child," describes Wendell's caring for his daughter by Kate. The child does not respond, however, and soon dies. Chapter 22, "And Amelia Sings a Lullaby," is a poem that is written in a kind of English street-ballad style. The song relates to the theme of the loss of a child after all the pain of delivery. This song, light and humorous, reflects Amelia's indifference to Kate's sorrow. The theme of the mystery of birth is carried into the following chapter, "Wendell Tells the Mystery to Julie and to Timothy." Again, a biblical style is used when Wendell explains the facts of life to his children.

From birth, the logical progression is to childhood; and in chapter 24, "Julie Becomes What She Had Read," the imaginative world of childhood is examined in a style that parodies nineteenth-century sentimental literature. Julie, who has been reading some saccharine children's books, has identified with Arabella Lynn, aged five, who one night comes downstairs to confess her sin of doubting God's existence. When she tossed up her adored ball, it came back down; and, if a God existed, He would surely have taken the treasure to heaven for His own use. She is tortured by the sin of doubting, and the next day she is dead. Now Julie-Arabella becomes the central figure of a sweet funeral with a hundred little girl mourners. But Julie (a wide reader) is no sooner laid in the earth than the heavens erupt a tempestuous sorrow of rainfall. Julie is cast into the marketplace to be sold with Jesus, but she moves from the New Testament to adolescent literature and becomes sweet sixteen. In her final fantasy, one apparently suggested by adult "cycle" novels such as John Galsworthy's *Forsyth Saga,* Julie becomes thoroughly bourgeois as she sees herself as an aged woman surrounded by her children who have themselves become adults.

In three chapters (26, 27, and 28) that occur before the midpoint of *Ryder,* the themes of prehistory, the realms of the Beast, and Myth, are explored in relation to modern man. A comic situation is used in chapter 26, "Kate and Amelia Go A-Dunging," when the two women clean the pigeon loft of its droppings and cast out the dead young. Amelia takes this occasion to observe that, when the earth was new, great primeval beasts paid back the earth solidly and richly with their droppings. Unlike the modern age of pigeons, the dung, in those days, amounted to something. In her vision of prehistory, Amelia sees great plants growing in a "tiger-pawed" earth. Time, too, she observes, seemed arrested; it "rotted on the stem of night and day. . . ."[18]

Just as chapter 26 reflects Amelia's thoughts about the prehistoric beast world, chapter 27, "The Beast Thingumbob," contains Wendell's story to his children that enlarges upon it. The Beast Thingumbob of his story falls in love with a mate who, like himself, had wings, fur, and feathers. One day she instructs her mate to take away her young, for she will die in childbirth. The beast does as directed but remains inconsolable about his loss, for "he knows her gift to him was the useless gift of love."[19] One dimension of this tale relates to the mythic past. For an "immortal," Thingumbob's mate actually lives 1,010 years and does die. Just as in mythology, the concept of immortality evolved from the struggle of the gods who, in overthrowing Chronos or Time, made Zeus (or Jupiter) the king of the gods in perpetuity; and, in this prehistoric situation, the term "immortal" is a qualified one. The mating of Thingumbob seems to tell of the male's uniting with the earth spirit to produce in his progeny the only real immortality.

The prehistoric vision of Amelia and Wendell's story of the mythic past are followed in chapter 28, "If Some Strong Woman—," by Doctor O'Connor's confession. A freak of nature, the doctor was born man but wishes to be woman. Doctor O'Connor does not speak of the mythic or legendary past. He does not, as in *Nightwood*, brag or dominate conversations. He serves well the women who are his principal patients, assisting them with care and with delicacy at their deliveries. When Amelia observes that so worthy a doctor deserves a good woman as a wife, the doctor, who bursts into tears, confesses that he has always wanted to be called "Hesper, first star of the evening."[20] The doctor has been betrayed by nature, even as Thingumbob's "immortal" mate dies in childbirth (supposedly part of a natural process), and even as time itself has betrayed the modern age with the puny pigeon droppings and killed the heavy beasts of an earlier and healthier era.

III *Midpoint of* Ryder

The midpoint (in the number of pages) of *Ryder* is reached in chapter 30, "The Cat Comes Out of the Well," which introduces the theme that brings the novel to its conclusion. Society is now encroaching upon the privacy of Wendell, for the public is outraged because his children do not attend school. Wendell had always avoided confrontations with society because of the frequency of his moves. At Bulls'-Ease (the Ryder farm) he is finally apprehended and called to a public hearing at the schoolhouse. The school, a dingy place, is cold, ill-furnished, and wretched. Wendell warns the officials that, as an outlaw, he is much easier to deal with than he would be as a respectable citizen. If they insist upon forcing his children to their school, he will demand that a new well be dug, since the present one contains three dead and decaying rats and a cat. Moreover, the words written in the privy will have to be erased and the school made as wholesome as his home. With these demands, Wendell purchases time.

In chapter 32, "The Soliloquy of Dr. Matthew O'Connor (Family Physician to the Ryders) on the Way to and from the Confessional of Father Lucas," Matthew's betrayal by nature into perversity is connected to a surrealistic vision of the church, and to the religious impulse, regarded as a kind of sexual black mass. Matthew confesses to Father Lucas (who is briefly mentioned also in *Nightwood*) that he has "done it" again, "and this time with Fat Liz, him as keeps bar in a gophered boudoir cap . . . ."[21] Father Lucas' admonitions to Matthew are distinctly two-faced; they lean heavily to homosexual double entendre. He tells O'Connor to sin no more, saying: "Visit me often . . . and I'll give you comfort and kind words and a little consolation that shall inch thee on thy way a bit . . . ."[22] Even more double-edged is Father Lucas' instruction that Matthew "cling to the pillar of righteousness, and shut thy mouth against the flesh of thy brothers whirled down the vortex of time, and lo! thou shall come to the peaceful lands where everything rises in still air, and the sun does not tremble and the planets are not mysterious, and the word goes forth from His Heart in a single uncorrupt stream and returns not, nor knows seasons in its mercy."[23]

The style switches abruptly from this playful scene to the surrealistic. In a vision of the church turned upside down, reality itself seems to slide; solids to melt. Candles rise to the ceiling, then wilt; the ceiling itself rises and descends; and this is followed by "fornication of the mass, parted and bred Death" a play on the "bread of life" of communion. The Savior, a life-giving image, is supplanted by "Death's wailing child in wax, lying in a bowl of wine, mouth open for the gushing breast of grief."[24] Matthew seems here to refer simultaneously to his brother Felix, dead of St. Vitus's disease, and to the death of Jesus as Savior. In this upside-down world, there can be no redemption.

Matthew's diction, with its Irish flavor, and his surreal vision of an inverted world (or the world of the invert) should be of especial interest to readers of *Nightwood;* for, while *Ryder* presents an earlier O'Connor, he is in some ways the same person in *Nightwood*. The Matthew of *Ryder* is, however, more "innocent" and a good deal younger. He looks at the world subjectively; but the O'Connor of *Nightwood*, now middle-aged, has learned to be more objective and his sufferings are endured in silence. On rare unguarded occasions, we see him slump; but he usually manages to hide his private woes behind a hearty manner. The later Matthew is also capable of deep response to the sufferings of others to which the earlier Matthew is partially blinded by his own subjectivity.

Chapter 34, "They Do Not Much Agree," is a mock-heroic parody of chivalric derring-do; but, instead of two knights on chargers battling for the honors of fair ladies, Amelia, mounted on Hisodalgus, and Kate, astride the red cow, come to an epic juncture over Wendell. They exchange compliments, such as "Goat-skin!" and "Pig's-bladder!" they tear off each other's clothes; and they bloody themselves. The comedy of action is replaced by the comedy of logic when Amelia cites her wifely and legal relationship to Wendell, only to have Kate counter that her own unwanted presence is responsible for Amelia's wisdom. The two women are reconciled, and Amelia promises to use her influence to stop Wendell from filling Kate with spices in his attempt to turn her into "Hot-Bottom."

In chapter 37, "Sweetly Told," Wendell has a visitor, Laura Twelvetree, whom he "entertains" in the music room while her husband sits outside meditating about mathematics. The comic device of a hand visible through a partly opened door is used several times. Laura gives Wendell a porcelain clock with only one hand; and Wendell passes it through the door. After Wendell makes love to Laura, a child's hand with a turquoise ring (by which Julie is identified) reaches in the door with the "india red fountain-of-all-ladies'-hope . . . a child's offering at the gate."[25]

The dramatic form is used for a comic sequence in chapter 41, "Wherein Sophia Goes A-Begging." The scene is the sanctum of a railroad magnate surrounded by twelve "disciples." Sophia, dressed as a pauper, addresses the magnate as "Boots," reminding him that she was once young and fair. Now she has a son, talented but weak, with "operas to his credit, with full orchestral directions planned, and executed amid the din of hungry children"[26] who are living on bread and water. Although the twelve suspect a fraud, Sophia departs with a goodly sum of money in her pocket.

IV *Denouement*

The final three chapters (48, 49, 50) of *Ryder* form a tying up of loose ends. Chapter 48, "Elisha in Love With the Maiden," sketches a hopeful future for one of Wendell's sons by Kate. As Elisha, aged fourteen, plays a Beethoven sonata on the piano, he looks at a picture of Beethoven, whose eyes remind him of Wendell. Elisha is the bastard son of Wendell; Wendell is the mythic father whose own conception (as reported by his mother) was immaculate because of her dream of Beethoven. Since Wendell is macrocosmic man, the earthly father is real; but he extends back into a primal past where beauty fuses with earthliness. Elisha ruminates on "love and the maiden" and on "death and the maiden" as he considers his musical future; for the piano is his mistress. In an imaginary trial, he is charged with being no more than a roadmender for the county. In his own defense, he replies that he will still play a concert in the town hall. Later, Elisha does perform with his work-hardened hands; they requite him; and he rises in tears to thunderous applause.

In chapter 49, "Three Great Moments of History," Doctor O'Connor is seen for the last time, and his fate too seems settled. For he catches a young lad legging it over the fence with a pot of honey he has just stolen from "Lady Drawbreeches." In an effort to turn the boy from the ways of crime, the doctor offers a short lesson in history, consisting of three "great moments" (a fourth will be added in *Ladies Almanack*). But the lessons are lost on the boy who is a poor scholar and fearful of death. The doctor and the youth confess to being nature's freaks, and they form an alliance.

In the final chapter, "Whom Should He Disappoint Now?," Wendell tells his mother that the law is now pressing most severely because he lives with two women and because his children are not attending the public school. He speaks to Kate about the problem; and Kate, histrionically brave, says she can support herself with her embroidery. When she begins to quote "dreadfully" from parts she once played when she was an actress, Wendell is so moved that he promises not to leave her. When Wendell tells Amelia that she must go, her position is that, since Wendell has always presented himself as a great man, what business has he to claim now that he is only "bloody mortal?" Sophia points out that Amelia can live with her brother; but, if Kate has to go, she has no one to take care of her; and Wendell's family has run out of money. Amelia agrees to leave.

When Wendell now goes into the night to sit among his animals and to ponder a solution, the refrain of this final scene is the chapter title's "Whom should he disappoint now?" Both of Wendell's women have already acquiesced to his needs. He has promised Kate never to leave her, and he has given Amelia by marriage a previous pledge to the same effect. "Whom should he disappoint now?" poses a question Wendell cannot answer, for he cannot choose. The night setting of this final scene—in which Wendell sits among the domestic animals, the mice, the night birds, and "creeping things"—offers a situation of potential evaluation and communion. But Wendell is unable, finally, to commune with the dumb beasts; the myriad eyes of night can only look at him, and he at them.

Ryder ends unresolved at the same point at which thirty years later Barnes takes up the family's history in *The Antiphon* although with different names and with a far more tragic treatment. Ryder, a tender man, is transformed into the more ruthless Bull Titus. The other family members, looked at half a century later, are also radically changed.

V *Social Criticism*

In substance, *Ryder* defies the conventions of Western society by inviting readers to favorably regard its central character, despite his weaknesses, and to look with distaste upon the organized, machinelike, prudish society which condemns him. The book argues, in effect, that, disjointed and peculiar as Ryder's life appears, it is closer to nature than more conventional lives; that such a life is more spontaneous, more joyous, and far more productive of beauty. This theme is sporadically conjoined with a plot from which it diverges when the author employs her art as illustrator, as poet, and as fabulist to stress her theme. The author, however, remains aware that Ryder's life is but one instance of the larger abstraction—how should man live? does modern man, especially, live validly? As a result, it has been necessary to approach a number of chapters of *Ryder* sequentially to establish the basic coherence of the entire work. What at first glance might appear to be random chapters of unrelated material—possibly humorous but inconsequential to the narrative—have been shown to be entirely integrated into a work in which the abstract quality, the theme, has from the beginning had preeminence over the plot.

No critical articles of *Ryder* have appeared since the initial reviews either praised or disparaged the novel. All the reviewers of 1928 were quick to attribute major influences and to point out Barnes's stylistic borrowings; yet not even the most flattering reviewers attempted to state the theme of the novel, to discuss the plot, or even to consider that it has both. Most were concerned with the author's stylistic flair; but, as an analysis of *Ryder* so abundantly makes clear, it is impossible to talk about Barnes's style and ignore the plot and the theme, or to discuss successfully the theme without reference to the various styles so carefully interfused with content.

However, as we have observed, this concern with style and this neglect of the overall organic quality of the novel were characteristic of the 1928 reviewers. The *New Republic* reviewer praised Barnes's literary gift in *A Book* but found *Ryder* too derivative in giving off "the dilute and echoed sound of Chaucer, Sterne and the King James Version."[27] No real attempt was made to deal with the plot or the theme, for the reviewer merely remarked that *Ryder* is a "tragedy of women"—a passing judgment very much open to argument. While the review is more complimentary in *The Nation*, it was no more helpful.[28] The reviewer saw the novel as an allegory, but failed to identify either the tale told or its allegorical meaning. Again, the style was seen as derived, this time from Chaucer, Sterne, Fielding, and James Branch Cabell. No doubt the reviewer was thinking of Cabell's *Jurgen* and the interrelationships of sex and knight errantry that are parodied in both *Jurgen* and *Ryder*.

Probably the most enthusiastic and detailed review came from Ernest Sutherland Bates in the *Saturday Review*,[29] but Bates' focus was upon Barnes's style. He utterly neglected the plot and the theme; indeed, when Bates wrote "Of plot interest there is little," he dismissed the entire structure of Ryder's family, his life and trials, and the import of the contest between hedonistic and civilized life-styles. Because of such vague reporting in the leading journals, we must wonder how *Ryder* sold successfully enough to go through two editions in one year. Still, Bates appreciated *Ryder* and praised its merits highly. He saw that the characters were "immortals" and were not intended to be portrayed in the realistic mode, thus answering a common complaint among reviewers that Ryder's characters are not "alive." Bates found Miss Barnes less erudite than Joyce, but he praised her style as "far more unified than his and far more virile." The most surprising judgment in this review is that *Ryder* is seen as "pornography, for its own amusing sake, exactly as it was with Aristophanes, Chaucer, Shakespeare, and Johnson and the other Elizabethans." We can only conclude that Bates's notions of pornography were very "soft," at least by today's standards.

The difference between the reviewer who wrote when *Ryder* first appeared and the critic who writes many years later is that the latter is addressing himself to an entirely different question than whether this book would interest readers sufficiently to purchase it. Today the critic sees *Ryder* in a continuum between short stories, one-act plays, and poems, on the one hand, and *Ladies Almanack*, *Nightwood*, and *The Antiphon* on the other. These titles constitute a body of work of developing skill and complexity in both style and thought. *Ryder*, then, is seen not as a potentially marketable and saleable book; rather, it is seen as de facto reality; it is an extravagant experiment in looking backward for stylistic models, while it looks at the same time at the contemporary world for its themes. It should be borne in mind that this book, bold by any standards, is a first novel; hence it is even more impressive for its abandonment of the author's already established and successful style (as seen in the short stories) and for its departure from the linear concept of the novel in which the organic quality is achieved through plot rather than through theme. *Ryder* is too intelligent, too entertaining, too well constructed to require apologists; all it requires is intelligent reading.

CHAPTER 5

Ladies Almanack

LADIES ALMANACK, a singular and unique short "novel," is a pretended compendium of lore about women who love women. Divided into twelve chapters, each is named for a month of the year. Patience Scalpel provides editorial comment, but the commentary is shared with the anonymous "Lady of Fashion" who claims authorship and who refers to herself at times in the first person and at others with the editorial "We." Patience Scalpel's humorous name describes the source of the book's comedy: a sharp tongue in a knowing, intelligent, and patient personality. The attitudes of both Patience and the "Lady of Fashion" contrast with the exaggerated behavior of this society of women, for these two female commentators share a common point of view, although the Lady of Fashion may be a bit milder in her remarks than Patience. Both women have admission to the lesbian society that the book describes, but both are observers. They present themselves as confounded and bemused by the profitlessness and the sterility of the sisterhood. Reference is made to Patience's experiences with men; and, when Patience herself swears that her daughters will marry, she is declaring her heterosexual preferences.

The mock-heroine of the *Almanack* is Dame Evangeline Musset, or "Saint Musset." Because she was powerfully attracted from an early age to girls, her father complained that she exhibited "most fatherly sentiments." As the months of the year comprise the chapters of the book, Dame Musset is young in "January"; by "November," she is fifty and filled with wisdom; by "December," she is dead at ninety-nine and her death and her absurdly elaborate funeral are described. Sylvia Beach identifies the model for Dame Musset as Miss Natalie Barney, a well-to-do woman who, in the Paris of the 1920s, kept a popular literary salon. Her house was particularly noted for its good food and for the presence of many feminists. Miss Barney was an enthusiastic horsewoman, and she frequently rode in the famous Paris park, the Bois de Boulogne. Indeed, at one point in the *Almanack*, Dame Musset is described as being "in a way an Amazon unhorsed . . . . " Miss Barney also served, according to Beach, as the presumed model for the "*Amazone*" of Remy de Gourmont's *Letters*. She is thought, as well, to have inspired the character of Valerie in Radcyliffe Hall's lesbian novel *The Well of Loneliness*, which argues, as Miss Beach put it, "that if inverted couples could be united at the altar, all their problems would be solved."[1]

I *Scenic Satire*

The question of marriage for lesbians is raised in chapter three, "March" of the *Almanack*, by two British women. Lady Buck-and-Balk and Tilly Tweed-in-Blood (a commoner, we suspect) journey to Paris to speak with Dame Musset about this very problem. They protest that the English law needs revision. Under the present law, two women who go to bed together are breaking the law. How, they demand, are they to get to heaven if they sin? Yet heterosexual couples are working their way to salvation with full civil and ecclesiastical sanction.

Matrimony for inverts is not, however, the theme of *Ladies Almanack*. Essentially, the book satirizes the absurdity of modern promiscuity among women, and it protests the absence of the decent restraints of privacy. Not only do women actively seek one another; they rather like to make public their various conquests; and the older mores of the past, when love implied commitment and faithfulness, are thereby undermined. Discretion no longer counts, the book complains; wisdom, too, is mocked in the streets since it proves too transient and changeable to be trusted and since no woman has respect for it.

Of plot, that is, the development of related events, there is none in *Ladies Almanack*. That element of story is replaced by the appearance of scenes, often only briefly described; and they are described or created because they are illustrative rather than because they are related to previous scenes. This device anticipates *Nightwood*, but in it there exists much more interrelating of the scenes.

Just as plot has been all but abandoned for scenic illustration, so the author presents her characters as non-individualized types.

Indeed, we have to remind ourselves that many of the characters are, in fact, modeled upon actual persons. Janet Flanner, in *Paris Was Yesterday*, identifies herself as one of a pair of lady correspondents, the Misses Nip and Tuck;[2] but no identifying characteristics appear in these heavily fictionalized types. The author's illustrations for the *Almanack* indicate her choice of type over character. As was the practice in *Ryder*, the *Almanack* is illustrated in the manner of the medieval illuminator, or limner. An essentially two-dimensional art of portrayal, this style stresses the visible surface of the object or person delineated instead of seeking to achieve the illusions of "depth" as in painting or of "depth of field" as in realistic photography.

For the *Almanack*, Barnes abandoned the styles used in *Ryder* for a more consistent diction. For the poetic novelist, an interdependency exists between the demands of the story to be told and the nature of the style in which the telling occurs. The *Ladies Almanack* celebrated the lesbian coterie of Paris in the late 1920s in a witty and salacious double entendre language. It is true that some parts of *Ryder*, particularly those in which Dr. O'Connor figure, employ some of the same devices; but the bulk of that work is better described as earthy rather than as off-color. *Ryder* draws the curtain over bedroom scenes, and the sexual escapades of its central character are alluded to or reported as if from some distance. *Ladies Almanack* comes much closer to being pornographic writing since specific sexual acts between women are frequently mentioned.

There is, as well, a difference in the motivation of the characters which influences the sexual quality of the two works. Ryder considered himself to be "appointed" to impregnate women, and the novel consistently presents Wendell as a spontaneous and innocent life force. He never appears to "lust after women," but he quite obviously does. Ryder is dealt with, that is, after his own lights; and he is accepted as sincere in his procreative self-appointment. The characters in *Ladies Almanack* are distinctly lustful; they are at least as promiscuous as Ryder and, despite their protestations of love, appear to seek gratification of their sexual appetites for pleasure alone. Thus Wendell's sense of biological purpose, together with the veiling of specific sexual deeds, modifies the novel's tone so that *Ryder* cannot be said to have the aim of arousing the reader's libidinal responses. Whether *Ladies Almanack* arouses such feelings obviously depends upon the nature of the reader, but the ingredients for arousal are clearly present. The nongenerative nature of the sexual activities tends to place the focus upon sex as pleasure, and that pleasure is even intensified by the forbidden (or at least socially deplored) delights of the woman-to-woman relationships that are depicted.

II *Wit and Humor*

The countervailing force to prurience in *Ladies Almanack* is apparent in Barnes's uses of wit and humor. An examination of the double entendre words and phrases—as well as the direct references to parts of the body or to lesbian sexual acts and responses—illustrate the ways in which the book achieves its flavor. Barnes's choices in vocabulary and phrasing are those of the past. Visibly Shakespearean are "parting is such sweet sorrow"; "if all's well, then ends well all ends up!"; and the pain of "Loveslabourlost." Hamlet's "It would cost you a groaning to take off mine edge"[3] to Ophelia may be implicit in Dame Musset's "the hone to my blunt."

Humorous names seem Shakespearean at times, for Barnes's Doll Furious reminds us of Doll Tearsheet in *Henry IV*, part 2. However, most names are probably more suggestive of the novel or comedy of Manners—the Duchess Clitoressa, Patience Scalpel, Senorita Flyabout, Haughty Moll, or Maisie Tuck-and-Frill. The alliteration in some names achieves a comic effect, as in Lady Buck-and-Balk, Tilly-Tweed-in-Blood, Bounding Bess, or Daisy Downpour. Of actual historical, biblical, or mythic names, few are masculine; there is mention only of Judas, Caesar, and John (Alden). As for historical women, those mentioned are Queen Anne, Priscilla (suggested to have preferred Jenny to John), Sheba, Sappho, and Catherine of Russia. Lady Macbeth is a Shakespearean reference, and from the Bible appears Jezebel. Penelope of Homeric legend occurs, and goddesses such as Juno and Venus receive mention.

The language used to refer to women includes relatively undateable terms like "baggage," "sluts," "Babes," "wench," "Madame," "girl," "lass," "crone," "scullion," and "Jade." But a woman is also described with coined words such as "sea-cattle," "land hogs," and "fish of earth." If they are lesbians, they are "Members of the Sect" or "one of us." Referred to adjectivally, they are "Cyprian," "Voltarian," or "Venereal." Their menstrual periods are alluded to conventionally as "changes," "moons," "months," "seasons," "distempers," and "equinoxes." But these periods are also "eclipses" (when love is impossible), "feminine tides," and occasions to "sit them on a stack of blotters."

The parts of a woman's body are sometimes likened naturalistically to those of stock animals, as in "hinder" and "fore" parts, "quarters," "haunch," "reins," "butt," "buttock," "flank," "joint," and "hip." But the female genitalia evoke a more imaginative language, examples of which include a "pansy field" (or "daffodil"), a "garden of Venus," a "pelt," a "Tarn of Temptation," or her "Jollies." Genitals can be hidden between two pillars, or they can be a "hollow tree," a "missing door," a "Windy space," the "cave's mouth," the "rowdy part," the "way-in," a "cow's trough," a "great gap," her "nothing," an "empty hack," a "toll-gate," a "turn-stile," a "door-lock," a "key-hole," or a "Breach-String-Alley." More conventionally, women's private parts are "Whorls and crevices," "organs," a "wallow," an "escutcheon," a "bush," a "nook," a "wound," a "spot," a "zone," an "Alley," a "path," a "ditch," a "burrow," or a "furrow."

Although no men appear in *Ladies Almanack*, male genitalia are mentioned when various substitutions of the phallus occur. Thus a woman may lack the "tools for the trade," but those are replaced by the "finger tip," the "tongue," the "nose-length," or the "underlip." The phallus is a "tool," a "beam," a "yard," a "sword." Women are born lacking "a trifle," an "inch," an "item." Men engage in the "carrying of coals" or "lifting of Beams," and they have "testicles" or "weights."

What one woman does with another appears in a number of fairly regular infinitive verbs—to "burn," "pinch," "bring," (to a "certainty"), to be "laid, thrown and branded"; to "wean"; to "floor"; to "lay on, charge and retreat," to "thaw," to "come," or "roost"; to "climb backward" or to "mislay"; to "Tamper with"; to "bring to rights"; to "spend oneself" to "Toledo"; to "blow bright"; to "foul"; to be "all thumbs"; to "bite the pippin," "ride," "trifle," or "come down upon." Noun phrases for acts between women include a "kneeling-to," a "Fal-lal," one's "true bite," and "slips of the tongue." Seen in these positions, women are "branch-to-branch," "bosom-to-bosom," "braid-to-Braid," "Womb-to-Womb"; they are a "trembling tandem," "Smack-of-astride," the "Rag-Tags of Sodom," the "flaps of Gomorrah," the "wash of the World."

Verbs and verb phrases show women as "spit" or "unspit" (or "unfathomed"); "bedded"; "haggard at both ends"; "melted"; or "my way hung." They are a "much thumbed mystery," a "rumpled meaning," "back mated," or "front to front," "high strung," or "low lying." They "go" and they "come," but only if they are "dated to a moon." The climax they experience is "the Oh!" when they are "brought forward," "to a certainty," "up to the standard," or as "Brooks to churning" when they experience a "beatitude" or "pain."

As these words, phrases and coinages suggest, a description of the style of *Ladies Almanack* is complicated by the fact that the vocabulary and the prose style do not necessarily derive from the same time periods. The verbal structures that we call sentences seem to be modeled upon the language of Manners as it occurs either in novels or in the comedies of Manners of William Wycherley, William Congreve, and other Restoration playwrights. The language is polished, urbane, witty, and worldly. The words and phrases used, however, are not really localized. We are not likely to find "scullion" today, but we do find "slut"; and, although either term was likely to occur at least as far back as Shakespeare's day, neither term can justifiably be called "Shakespearean." The author's hyphenated coined words are equally undatable; they are most frequently created from a vocabulary available as far back as the beginning of Middle English.

This unaccustomed use made of standard words is at the heart of Miss Barnes's innovative use of language. "Venereal" is so commonly used that we have to remind ourselves that the adjective derives from Venus; but "Voltarian" and "Cyprian" are both less common adaptations of the proper noun to the uses of the adjective. The metaphoric approaches of the poet transform the meanings of ordinary words to achieve startling effects. Thus common nouns—"ditch," "burrow," "alley," "wound"—when they are used as metaphors for the private parts acquire overtones of harshness or softness of a hiding place, of a public place, of an injured place, or of simply *The* Place as in "spot."

Stylistically, *Ladies Almanack* advances the author's facility with prose fiction beyond the developments apparent in *Ryder*. In *Ryder*, Barnes's talent for parody of older literary styles is evident, but her skill is admittedly used for imitative purposes. *Ryder's* handling of plot and theme as separate and thus susceptible to being advanced independently is certainly not imitative. Moreover, this conception of the writing of fiction is heightened significantly in *Ladies Almanack* where the disjunction between plot and theme gives to the theme an overriding significance; as a result character and situation become merely illustrative.

By the time Miss Barnes began writing *Nightwood*, she was not only familiar with an extended work of fiction; she was in fact already accustomed to conceiving its adaptability to her own tendency to prefer thematic lines over story lines. She was an innovator and experimenter with that longer fictional form, and she had also become quite adept in separating vocabulary from sentence style. She had shown her inventiveness with vocabulary in *Ryder* and in *Ladies Almanack*, but she had settled for a prose style that was still largely borrowed from the seventeenth- and eighteenth-century dramatists and novelists of Manners. If *Nightwood* was to be a major achievement, she would have to combine her already well-developed skills with a departure in the form of the sentence itself—from her earlier parodic forms to a new prose, one distinctive and characteristically her own.

CHAPTER 6

Nightwood: *The Poetic Novel*

IN *Ryder* and *Ladies Almanack* method of narration, the diction, and organization are appropriate to their subjects; in *Nightwood* the achievement is also unique: the prose narrative form is fused with poetic diction, and both are shaped to meet the demands of the story. The story of *Nightwood* traces the impact upon four people—Felix Volkbein, Nora Flood, Jenny Petherbridge, and Dr. Matthew O'Connor—of a fifth character, Robin Vote, who passes through their lives as in a dream but affects each in ways that are achingly real. Of these five major characters, four are American and one European. All are expatriates living in Paris, where most of the action occurs. A brief flashback at the beginning of the novel takes us to a scene in Vienna; two others occur in Berlin; and the climax occurs somewhere in upstate New York.

Robin Vote, the young American girl, is the actual protagonist of the novel; for, whether or not she is physically present, her influence compels and directs all significant actions, speeches, pronouncements, curses, and descriptions. Her immense power over others is unwilled, unconscious, and even indifferent. All things to others, she is as nothing to herself. Unable to help herself or to be helped, she is tragically frozen between two worlds: the human and the bestial.

I "*Bow Down*"

The opening chapter establishes the premise that "truth" is ahistorical. Felix Volkbein, born in 1880, is the son of an Italian Jew, Guido, and of a Viennese Christian, Hedvig, who dies in childbirth. From Guido, who died before Felix was born, Felix inherited the fictitious title of Baron Volkbein, Guido's desire to be accepted in society, and a certain innate ability to prosper. A "Wandering Jew,"

Felix surfaces from unknown places and activities at age thirty, whereupon he begins to create a "past" for himself from the family legends his aunt reports, and with the two portraits of actors who Felix pretends are portraits of his parents. He speaks seven languages, and he earns a substantial income by his ability to manage and invest money.

The "present" of *Nightwood* is established as 1920, when Felix is forty years old. Although his business takes him to other countries, he is living in Paris. Felix stands outside of "historical" life; although he has nominally become a Christian, the ancient prejudices against Jews are still very much in force; and, as a result, the society to which he aspires is closed to him. He loves the concepts of royalty and nobility, and he tends to "Bow Down" ever so slightly to persons who may be titled. Since he is unable, because of his race, to enter that prized "historical" world, Felix does the next best thing: he becomes associated with a world of make-believe titles in an industry whose product is make-believe. He comes to know many people in the entertainment world, notably the theater and the circus; and, like himself, his friends assume the fictitious titles of "Baron," "King," "Principessa," "Princess," and, the "Duchess of Broadback." Through the "Duchess," a particular friend, Felix has the opportunity to meet a count (whose title is also spurious); and at the "Count's" home he becomes acquainted with Dr. Matthew O'Connor and Nora Flood, two of the novel's main characters.

Nora's role is that of a neutral observer, and the main focus of this chapter is upon an interchange which occurs between Felix and Dr. O'Connor, as the latter "holds forth," dominating the conversation with his own monologue. Felix is drawn naturally enough into this conversation, for the doctor expresses a point of view that is opposite his own. The doctor insists that the "truth" of man lies not in his history, but in legend; history is merely the record of the public lives of public figures. Their private lives are censored out of written history; but legend, the doctor explains, is "unexpurgated." The real issue of this meeting is its impact upon Felix, for the doctor's disdain for history is a revelation for him. He becomes, in fact, uncontrollably emotional; at first he laughs and then he cries out as if under unbearable stress. The doctor (not a licensed practitioner; his title is also spurious) later reveals to the duchess an intuitive understanding of something incomplete about Felix. In some way he is "damned from the waist up."

II *"La Somnambule"*

Just as Felix's inability to enter the larger world of history prepared him to accept as substitute the milieu of the circus's "underworld" performers as friends, so this world prepares him for his friendship with Dr. O'Connor, who is truly of the "night world" of legend. And Felix's friendship with the doctor prepares him for Robin Vote. Through the doctor, Felix first sees Robin; and the doctor's impact upon Felix's thinking prepares him to consider Robin as his wife.

As Felix and the doctor discuss their friendship, the doctor observes that the Jew and the Irishman are much alike; if the Jew traditionally suffers, the Irish have "creative misery." But their conversation makes clear that the nature of the suffering that the two friends experience is not the same. Felix, with his compulsion to view the world historically in terms of great names and events, suffers outwardly; for he is without a social place. The doctor, unconcerned about "place," suffers inwardly from a too great cognition that he is out of phase with the human race. His is the greater despair. The doctor thinks of himself as a woman. Although middle-aged, he has never become used to his own beard. He carries his hands pawlike before him, and he is spiteful toward men who ignore him. He is effeminate and at times "bitchy."

A summons to a nearby hotel brings the doctor and Felix to the bedside of Robin Vote who has apparently fainted. An authorial comment indicates that Robin is a "born somnambule"; she has not so much fainted as she has fallen into a strange, consuming sleep.

This first appearance of Robin is important both thematically and poetically. Robin lies on her bed as in an "arranged" composition. Although she wears trousers and pumps and seems to be arrested in the midstep of a dance, she is surrounded by evidences of the jungle. Palms, plants, and flowers proliferate around her; and birds, neglected in their cages, sing. In the middle of the city, she has created for herself an environment that reflects her instinctual nature.[1] Left unattended, she might not be able to rouse from this deep sleep, for she emits the phosphorescence of decay—a kind of luminous aureole illuminates her head.

The doctor manages a partial revival by flinging water in Robin's face, while Felix stands, an unseen observer, behind the potted palms. An unusual energy possesses the doctor as he attends to Robin, partly because, as unlicensed practitioner, he fears apprehension by the police, and partly, it appears, because the atmosphere of a woman's boudoir charges him with a kind of empathic fire. He is at once magician, witch doctor, and woman. He makes certain gestures, "honesties,"[2] like those of the magician; and, under the cover of these movements, he applies Robin's perfume to himself, uses her powder puff, colors his lips with her rouge. He also appropriates a one-hundred franc note that is lying in sight, an act also observed by Felix, who is learning that to be a friend involves a good deal of forgiving.

Robin is described as "beast turning human." Her eyes seem inhuman; her movements and way of walking are both "headlong" and "sideways," "clumsy" and "graceful." She seems to walk instinctively, like animals. Felix is evidently attracted immediately by Robin; for, when asked by the doctor of what nationality he would choose a wife, he answers promptly that she would be an American. Felix begins courting Robin by introducing her to his own preoccupation with history. After she involuntarily accepts his proposal and marries him, Felix takes Robin to Vienna and vainly attempts to interest her in the great names and events of his birthplace. But Felix is obliged to abridge the honeymoon when he realizes that Robin is paying no attention to him. In the months that follow, while they are living in Paris, he persists with his infatuated notion of engaging Robin's interest in the past, only to discover that she typically falls asleep while he is talking. Finally Felix demands to know why they have not had a child, for from the start it has been his dream to father a son who would cherish the glories of history as he does. Robin submits to motherhood as offhandedly as she married. But, when Robin becomes pregnant, she begins to wander about, even taking trains to distant places. She converts to Catholicism and visits churches. But the nuns she talks with soon learn what Felix has come to realize—Robin is living prehistorically in some time so ancient that the very concepts of sin and absolution have not yet been invented. As a result, she can be helped by neither religion nor history.

When Robin prays, trying to think of her unborn son's future, she discovers that her mind has wandered instead to consideration of the women of history and literature. She thinks of Catherine of Russia, Madame de Maintenon, Catherine de Medici, Anna Karenina, and Catherine Heathcliff. Robin's prayers are "monstrous," for they are mere self-preoccupations: she worries, for example, that she may be still growing; for Robin is already tall, and she has a boy's body. Robin is delivered of a small and sickly son who is almost a fulfillment of Dr. O'Connor's prophetic remark that "the last child born to aristocracy is sometimes an idiot."[3] But, by giving birth Robin is not transformed into a mother. A week after the delivery, she is "lost." She takes more and more to wandering; she is, in fact, seldom home. Felix is unable to locate her or to know what to do when he does. He occasionally sees her bent over her drink in a bar, for Robin has by this time taken to considerable drinking. She manages to resist the impulse, on one occasion, to dash her child against the floor. Finally, she tells Felix she did not want a child; she would have its existence kept a secret. She soon leaves Felix and the child, and she literally disappears.

III *"Night Watch"*

After abandoning her home, Robin had evidently left Paris for America, where she lived for some while before meeting Nora in the fall of 1923, or three years after Felix's meeting with Robin.

Nora is introduced in a rural American setting that seems as appropriate to her as Robin's junglelike room was to her. Just as the previous chapter dealt with the rise and fall of Felix's relationship with Robin, "Night Watch" carries the love between Robin and Nora from its beginning to its abridgement. Nora, an advance agent for the Denckman Circus, lives in her ancestral family home, one that dates back to pre-Revolutionary days. There she entertains an odd and undifferentiated assortment of "poets, radicals, beggars, artists and people in love."[4] She is an "historical" person, much like Felix; but, where Felix longs for a measure of participation in history and is denied, Nora is an historical personage without so much as giving the fact a thought. She is by temperament a fundamentalist, "savage and refined"; like Robin, she is preoccupied with herself; and, like Robin's smile, hers is one on the surface and bitter.

The two women meet at the Denckman circus in New York where they happen to take adjoining ringside seats. When the animals pass around the ring, they are powerfully attracted to Robin, a tendency that is climaxed when a great lioness, instead of moving around the ring, lies down before Robin, her paws extended through the bars. An intense animal sympathy is established between Robin and the jungle beasts by the huge cat's spontaneous response to a woman who is somehow a sister. But is the lioness's sorrow for her own captivity or for Robin's outcast state? Hovering as she does between the human and bestial worlds, Robin seems the more to be pitied of the two. The upshot of this strange moment is that Robin rises to leave, and at the same instant is seized by Nora, who intervenes to "savc" Robin. Robin is still as lost as she was after the birth of her son, Guido.

In an effort to provide a home, Nora takes Robin to Munich, Vienna, Budapest, and finally Paris where she buys an apartment. The time of their living together is described in one short paragraph: the relationship is no sooner established than it begins to disintegrate. Robin soon resumes her wandering; and she returns home, if at all, only after a night spent with people of all sorts in the bars and cafés of Paris. Like Felix, Nora finds that she can neither comfortably go to these places with Robin nor bear to confront her in them.

Nora finally settles into a life of waiting and hoping for Robin's return. This relationship persists for the better part of four years; in 1927, Jenny Petherbridge, to whom Nora is to lose Robin, meets Robin. Nora gradually realizes that, though Robin is still living with her, she has already passed out of her life; she remains as only an "intaglio" kept alive by Nora's own blood. Like Felix, Nora learns that Robin cannot be kept, contained, or even lured to inhabit a home.

A dream prefigures Nora's loss of Robin. The dreamer attempts to place Robin in some kind of historical perspective, for in the dream Nora invites Robin to Nora's grandmother's forbidden room, only to discover that the room is not really her grandmother's. Moreover, her grandmother is dressed in a sort of ringmaster's costume, complete with "billycock and a corked mustache, ridiculous and plump in tight trousers and a red waistcoat."[5] The leering ringmaster-grandmother incestuously connects with Nora's fears for Robin—that she too is being seduced in some terrible way.

Upon awakening from this dream, Nora, in her restless pacing, is brought to see Robin and Jenny in the garden. Jenny is clinging to Robin's neck next to the granite statue of a woman. Nora is as one struck down by the sight and by the momentary meeting of hers and Robin's eyes. Yet this most terrible betrayal of all is somehow tempered by Nora's perception that Robin will remain "safe," for she will always pass, without effort, from one woman's arms to another's.

IV *"The Squatter"*

By a kind of degenerative progression, main characters are introduced in successive chapters as falling farther and farther away from the initial truth of life as legend. Dr. O'Connor voiced a large and fairly objective view of "world life" in the first chapter when he argued that man's true history is legendary. He awakened Robin and projected her into the novel as a living force. But his awakening was an objective, or "safe" gesture; it did not really touch his own person. Felix, whose preoccupation is history, also tends to take a large view of life but one not so objective. His grasp of history is marred by his subjective desire to fit himself into that history; and, as a result, he marries Robin and fathers her child upon whom he places his own ambitions. Unlike the doctor, who tries to stand aside from both history and legend, Felix is personally committed to his vision.

Nora is introduced in the chapter "Night Watch" as an historical person with a two-hundred-year tradition. But Nora's thoughts are certainly not about history. She lives subjectively within her own desires and is quite unconscious of either the legendary world view the doctor advances or the historical vision of man seen in Felix. Yet Nora has personal integrity and a personal commitment outside of Self—her love for Robin—which endows Nora with human significance. With her human responses and her capabilities of fidelity and love, Nora is the least eccentric, the most "normal," of *Nightwood*'s characters. With the introduction of Jenny Petherbridge in the fourth chapter, the question arises whether Jenny should be considered from the perspective of legend, history, or humanity.

When Jenny is first seen in Nora's garden, she is clinging to Robin's neck; and she steals Robin away like a thief in the night. Jenny, who is vainly preoccupied with history, has worried four husbands into their graves by trying to live vicariously through them; and she now has the accumulated wealth of those four men with which to fulfill her ambitions. Jenny, who is incapable of any authenticity whatever, is called a "squatter" because her entire life, both material and immaterial (we hesitate to use the word "spiritual"), is secondhand. The photo of Robin on Jenny's table was taken for Nora; she wears a wedding ring, one not her own; her books have been selected for her by others; and even her vocabulary is "loaned." Accursed by ambition, Jenny is forever tense and expectant. Her very emotions ring false, for she falls in love "with a perfect fury of accumulated dishonesty."[6]

Jenny's motivation for stealing Robin from Nora is not derived from her passion for Robin but from the fact that Nora's is the most passionate love she knows. Jenny's grasping but petty piracy is suggested in early meetings with Robin where, at a restaurant table, Jenny is seen ludicrously leaning so far across the table that she must twist her ankles around the chair rungs to keep from falling; Robin, meanwhile, leans back in a parallel, leaning plane, her own legs drawn back for support. This figure of frozen imbalance is resolved in a toppling tableau at the end of the chapter.

"The Squatter" does not follow chronologically the previous chapter; rather, it recounts the way Jenny stole Robin away from Nora and brings the novel's time to the same moment that ended the previous chapter: to that scene in the garden when Jenny clung to Robin's neck. The narrative portion of "The Squatter" describes events on the evening at the opera when Dr. O'Connor introduces Jenny to Robin. The doctor comes to Jenny's house, as does Robin, after this meeting. Quite a few people are present, and among them is an old marchesa who follows astrology and who predicts that Robin has come to her final incarnation. Jenny and Robin are alter egos, the opposite halves of the human personality in its most extreme forms. Robin is the beast turning human; Jenny is the "accident" that has somehow turned an individual into a beast—or "the accident that made the beast the human endeavor."[7] Robin is neither the beast turning human (she is unsuccessful, finally, in being either human or beast), nor the fulfillment of the marchesa's prophesies. Rather, Robin exists between two worlds, human and bestial; and, by the end of the novel, she is frozen, "immortalized," in that limbo state.

Still, the mention of what appears to be Robin's final incarnation is upsetting to Jenny, who orders the carriages so the party can go out for some air. Unable to handle situations and incredibly jealous, Jenny is really calling for the carriages in order to prohibit conversation. When Jenny goes to dress, Robin notes that she is upset, is "in a panic," and will dress "in something old."[8] Thus Robin innocently betrays herself, for how would she know these habits of behavior and dress if she had just this night met Jenny, as the doctor supposes? He does not know that at the time of his "introduction," about which he later feels so guilty, Jenny had known Robin for a year. That Jenny will dress in "something old" echoes Robin's predilection for making her own dresses out of the old material that she finds in secondhand shops, and reinforces the backward-looking tendency of the prehistoric person. Robin looks at old materials because she is spontaneously attracted to them, but Jenny dresses in an old hoop skirt because she seeks to make herself attractive to Robin and thus to compensate for her own insecurities.

Jenny's costuming has no effect on Robin, who is talking with the child Sylvia when Jenny reappears. Sylvia has responded to Robin as automatically as the circus animals have. Moreover, an English girl is also attracted to Robin; and, as the party approaches the carriages, it is clear that Robin and the English girl are about to sit together and ignore Jenny. Jenny's strident calling manages to get Robin into her carriage, but at the price of the unwanted presence of both the English girl and Sylvia. Squeezed in with them is the doctor (who must be "witness" to this scene for later narrative purposes).

As the carriages move through the Bois de Boulogne, the doctor speaks in a veiled fashion of his own longing to be a woman. He has apparently just been embroiled in some sort of trouble, for he has spent the past twenty-four hours in jail. To the doctor's remarks, Jenny replies with a strident and demanding "What?" or "what, what is that you say?"[9]; but she is actually directing her speech at Robin in an ineffectual attempt to separate her from the English girl. Finally brought to tears, Jenny speaks of her love as being finer than a man's, as being "sacred" and "great." Robin is moved to tell Jenny, at length, to "shut up." At this point, the frozen tableau of the restaurant is completed. Jenny begins to claw at Robin, who sinks unresistingly to the carriage floor. Jenny then falls upon Robin, and begins to beat her. The child Sylvia is petrified by fear. Robin leaps from the carriage as it stops before Nora's apartment, and runs into the garden. Jenny follows, and we are told that, shortly after, Robin and Nora separated and that Jenny took Robin to America.

Although four chapters remain in the novel and well over half its total pages are yet to be experienced, Robin is not seen again until the final short coda chapter, "The Possessed." Although she is spoken of and although she directs the events of the remainder of the book as surely as if she were physically present, a good measure of the achievement of *Nightwood* is precisely this economy in the use of the protagonist. The peculiar charm of Robin is her strangeness; she is invested with a remoteness and a restless questing (as though she were seeking but not finding her own kind). She is beautiful, as even the doctor admits, but nothing is made of her physical beauty, although a good deal is made of her ungainly grace. Nor is her bisexuality important; for others, such as Jenny, are bisexual. Nor can it be said that Robin is particularly unpredictable. Lacking a will, she is moved by others and dominated by them.

A point that Faulkner made in *The Mansion* is applicable to Robin. Faulkner's two most beautiful women are Eula Varner Snopes and her daughter Linda. Both are in part shaped by Faulkner's reading of Djuna Barnes.[10] Eula is glorified to the level of myth; she is a Helen, a Semiramis. Linda, shell-shocked into deafness, becomes for Faulkner the feminine beauty and the perfection that approach the ideal. And a good part of Linda's beauty (it is a "literary" beauty) is her silence. Since she cannot hear herself speak, she cannot control her voice; and she prefers instead to communicate by writing notes. In the development of Linda, Faulkner observes that Helen of Troy never spoke; at least no single recorded syllable exists of her speech, although she no doubt spoke as much as any other woman. Speech would necessarily have had to do with the mundane things of daily living: matters of household responsibility that do not lend themselves to a universalized image of ideal feminine beauty. While Robin frequently sings and talks in bars to perfect strangers, making her way from table to table, her words are unrecorded. Seldom quoted in relation even to the major characters of *Nightwood*, Robin's silence underscores her strange and remote beauty.

V "*Watchman, What of the Night?*"

The fifth chapter, "Watchman, What of the Night?" is essentially a poetic soliloquy on the nature of the night. Having lost Robin, Nora realizes that she never understood the world to which Robin belongs. In the middle of the night, she climbs the six floors of an apartment building to the tiny room Dr. O'Connor rents. As she enters, she sees an incredibly squalid scene: women's underclothes hang from the bureau drawers; rouges and other cosmetics stand upon the bureau amid medical instruments, rusty forceps, a broken scalpel; books are piled anywhere; and there is a swill pail "brimming with abominations."[11] In the bed, the doctor is wearing a nightgown and a wig of long blonde curls; his cheeks are rouged; and he has painted his eyelashes. Nora is startled; but the doctor, after whipping off his wig, accepts the situation and his discovery. These events represent all the plot of this rather long chapter, for the remainder is given to the doctor's attempt to allay with words Nora's loss of Robin.

The night is, we are told, the doctor's favorite theme. He tells Nora that all nights are different but that those in France are best. The Americans, with their cult of cleanliness, have washed away their own instinctual tracks; the French, indifferent to dirt, retain their orientation between the day and night. Sleep, love, and death all belong to the night; and, to make matters difficult, each person has another identity during the night: one which constitutes a betrayal of waking values. Living continently, for example, invites betrayal. In dreams we discover ourselves in the beds of lovers we had never even considered, while our own true love in sleep moves her legs apart for an army—or murders us. Since these dream figures have no known address, no names, they must be ourselves, a part of our unknown identity. Implicit in the doctor's thesis is the necessity for recognizing that our identities are not what we think they are.

For Nora, the doctor's portrayal of the night constitutes a redefinition of reality; but reality is now seen in tragic terms that especially stress man's helplessness because of his own unknown nature. What holds true for male homosexuals is also true for women who should have been men: they too are irrevocably committed to the night; they too haunt the *pissoirs* and curse physical liabilities. About the only solace for the lonely invert is achieved by way of a sense of humor and by the thought that age gradually enfeebles. Finally, death, or at least its promise, brings relief. Night people more than others, he suggests, exist in a living death.

The doctor admits that he works at "cross-purposes," for his words are only a futile attempt to solace Nora. At length, he recapitulates the evening at the opera when he "introduced" Jenny to Robin, and his description of Jenny echoes with wit and compassion the one already given in "The Squatter." Jenny, approaching fifty, evokes pity in the doctor. In meeting Robin, she is unexpectedly boosted up to the "banquet" of life; but, in introducing Jenny and

Robin, Matthew knows he is betraying his friendship for Nora. Still, he points out, who will not betray others as well as himself for food and drink? The doctor recounts the invitation to Jenny's, the costuming Jenny resorted to (although he incorrectly describes her as having been so dressed at the opera), and the carriage ride that ends on Nora's street. He ends by observing that he was conscious, at the moment of violence, that the true passion was Nora's for Robin: "Nora will leave that girl some day; but though those two are buried at opposite ends of the earth, one dog will find them both."[12] This last remark serves as dramatic anticipation for the ending of the novel when Nora's dog does indeed find Robin and summons Nora by his barking. Thus "Watchman" ends by providing the third perspective of the events that concluded chapters three and four.

VI *"Where the Tree Falls"*

The sixth chapter, "Where the Tree Falls," centers around Felix's son Guido, although the child is entirely passive and is given no dialogue; and the year must be 1931, for Guido is ten years old. Guido, who wears heavy lensed glasses, is "Mentally deficient and emotionally excessive, an addict to death."[13] Guido wants to enter the church, for he is as strongly inclined to religion as his father is toward history. Although Felix doubts whether Guido will ever be accepted by the church, he prepares to move to Vienna where, if Guido's religious calling fructified, he would be among his own people. As a result of Felix's problems and plans, Felix's dinner invitation to Dr. O'Connor is an opportunity to discuss his difficulties, and to take leave of his friend. In uprooting himself for his son, Felix is aware that he is fulfilling Guido's wishes but destroying his own hopes. It is apparent to Felix that Guido will never marry and become a father; and, in accepting this knowledge, Felix accepts the devastation of his own hope for a place in history. Still other considerations worry him: he confesses to the doctor that he never understood Robin, and he is also concerned over the shock to Guido's system that Jenny ruthlessly perpetrated on her recent visit to Felix's home.

Felix tells the doctor about the curious visit paid him by Jenny; but, since her motive for the incident is never really explained, the reader must supply it as best he can from his knowledge of Robin. Ostensibly, Jenny came to Felix to buy a painting; but Felix could see that she had really come to speak about Robin. Part of an explanation that must surely be valid is Jenny's bitchiness: her desire to inflict unnecessary pain. For little Guido is present in the room all the while Jenny describes the behavior of this unknown and strange woman who is finally identified as his own mother. But the reader, knowing Robin, is able to supply an even more likely motivation for Jenny's visit. The details she offers suggest that Robin has again taken to the wandering she had done when she lived with Felix and later with Nora, and Jenny suggests Robin's many betrayals of affection. In all likelihood, Jenny suspects that she is losing Robin and wants to transmit her pain to others.

Jenny "staged" this encounter with Felix by dressing in what Robin would call "something old" but what Felix calls making her "toilet rusty and grievous."[14] And, despite all her histrionics, Jenny only tells Felix that Robin lets her pets die and recounts an instance of Robin's fickleness. The child Sylvia had stayed some while with Jenny and had fallen in love with Robin, who awoke the child repeatedly at night to reassure herself of Sylvia's love. After the child's departure, Jenny wonders whether Robin "had a heart" (thus suggesting that Robin has indeed taken to wandering at night into the arms of other women). Jenny then brings Sylvia back to her home during the holidays as an experiment. While Jenny denies she "used" the child, she did; for she succeeded, as she intended, to prove that Robin no longer remembered Sylvia. Jenny has timed her performance before Felix in order to arrive at the door for her exit line: "Robin . . . Baronin Robin Volkbein; I wonder if she could be a relative."[15]

Guido is made suddenly ill by this news, and Felix turns all his attention to the child. Felix, it is clear, very much loves his son and, through his son, Robin. Guido's neck is Robin's, and the depraved "innocence" of Robin is transmuted into a real innocence in Guido. But the doctor, having heard Felix's story, insists upon redefining the concept of depravity: truly perceived, it is but "the sense of the past . . . most fully captured."[16] "Ecstasy, religion and love," he continues, all partake of the nature of ruin and corruption. Unlike most people, Robin was unafraid of either destiny or history.

Questions follow rapidly, as the doctor attempts to assuage Felix's troubled mind. In Guido, he assures Felix, he has found what all men seek: calamity. Felix has lived with a preoccupation for history; thus in a sense he denied an entire dimension of his own personality. But in Guido, who trembles on the verge of religious ecstasy,

Felix's unacknowledged self is made manifest in the flesh. Guido's religious disposition partakes of man's irrational and intuitive nature, and thus of a more "legendary" kind of truth than that seen in linear history. This associative relationship which locates parts of the Self in others is also seen in the doctor, who regards himself as a good Catholic and who evidently is seen (according to a rumor Jenny purveyed to Felix) a good deal in the convent, where he is supposed to attend "illegal" cases in return for free meals. And his alienation from a fully integrated Self is also seen in the following chapter, when the doctor is in church.

The doctor reassures Felix about Guido's mentality by saying that Guido's mind, an unknown factor, may carry greater potential than a known mind. The doctor parries Felix's final question about whether or not Robin was "damned" by replying that Guido is "blessed—he is peace of mind."[17] The baron acknowledges the possibility that both Robin and Guido are "a little mad" but he is able to accept this possibility as the price for their unique ability to read the heiroglyphics of, respectively, the past and the future.

Felix, Guido, and Frau Mann (the "Duchess of Broadback") are seen arriving at Vienna at the end of the chapter. Both Felix and Frau Mann, who are by now heavy drinkers, take Guido with them as they make the rounds of cafés. Felix spends his money readily to hear German music, and he attends affectionately to his son. But he is incorrigible to the end; he bows to a figure in a cafe who, Felix has persuaded himself, is no other than the Grand Duke Alexander of Russia. A foolish gesture, almost involuntary, perhaps, it only cements in Felix's own mind the madness of his preoccupation with visible greatness. Felix's final act as the chapter ends is one of attention to Guido; he warms the child's hands. The scene is the last one the reader sees of Felix and Guido.

VII *"Go Down, Matthew"*

In the chapter "Go Down, Matthew," the doctor pays a return call on Nora. Since Nora's surprise visit to Matthew's room, they have become closer acquaintances. Nora, aware of Matthew's secret transvestite identity, knows that the doctor considers himself responsible for Nora's loss of Robin; and the doctor realizes that Nora is inconsolable. She cannot stop thinking of Robin, remembering her, loving her, writing her endless letters. Robin, now in America, has forgotten Nora, as she forgets everything. The doctor's futile purpose in visiting Nora is to argue her into abandoning her memory of Robin. But, rather than bring her relief about Robin, he only succeeds in identifying himself so closely with her suffering that he drives himself to distraction.

The doctor's point is that life is suffering and that suffering does not end; pain in no way carries the correlation that relief must be forthcoming. Most people, he points out, marry to get through life; but Nora is wedded to her own suffering. He illustrates the tenacity of Memory and the longing for innocence with a description of the "tuppenny uprights ," or "ladies of the *haute* sewer,"[18] who, having aged in their profession, make their last stand under London Bridge. Though they hold up their flounces and "do it" standing, they are still waiting innocently for the promises of their own long-gone childhood. And the doctor admits to having seen the priest about his own longings. Father Lucas told the Doctor that "just being miserable isn't enough—you have got to know how." Taking his advice, Matthew sought out a small church and confronted his own problem. He exposed "Tiny O'Toole" to God's scrutiny, but Tiny remained "in a swoon." Since shaming his own impotency did no good, Matthew recognized that he was a "permanent mistake" and that no miracle occurs in the church.

Innocence and corruption are viewed by Nora and the doctor as the obverse of one another. Both the person with a strong identity and he with little, for example, feel they can do no wrong. Thus the doctor's sex is an accidental distinction of identity imposed upon him by nature.

Nora recounts her breakup with Robin. After Nora's conversation with the doctor in "Watchman, What of the Night?" Nora went to see Jenny. In Jenny's home, Nora saw the photograph of Robin as a child that Robin had told Nora was lost. And she saw on the bed a doll Robin had given Jenny, just as she had once given one to Nora. Since this doll is their "baby," Nora knew that Robin and Jenny were lovers. As a result of this meeting, Nora told Robin that their relationship was over.

Nora recounts a scene prior to the breakup that sketches in the shape their life together had taken. Nora had followed Robin one night. Robin was drunk, and she let herself at such times be handled by anyone. When Nora had tried to extricate her from an interested crowd of bystanders, she had only managed to precipitate a scene; for Robin had accused Nora of making her feel "dirty and tired and old." Police and others gathered about; and when Nora walked away, Robin ran after her shouting accusations until they came upon an old and bedraggled whore. Robin insisted that Nora give the woman money; then Robin sat in the dirt and petted her. Nora finally got Robin home; but she realized that the only time she could really possess Robin was when she was drunk.

The real crime of *Nightwood*—as well as the real cause of the breakup between Robin and Nora—was not, however, such night scenes. The crime was committed by Nora herself when she slapped the sleeping Robin into consciousness and out of that strange nightworld to which she had returned. An instantaneous effect was perceptible in Robin who seemed to Nora to become corrupt and to wither away before her eyes. As Nora recounts the events of their life together, she is actually trying to keep alive by the sheer strength of her emotions that which is already dead: the relationship she had herself destroyed. She comes to see that she had loved Robin not for Robin's sake but for her own: "Matthew . . . have you ever loved someone and it became yourself?"[19]

The effect of Nora's suffering upon the doctor is disastrous. He has, he tells Nora, long since given up cherishing a sense of self; but he had felt "safe" in his identification with his friends. Now, through his sympathies with Nora, his defenses have been broken; and he is exposed to suffering. But Nora is not yet through using Matthew as the vessel into which she pours her grief. Although Robin wanted to be gay, and also wanted everyone else to be, this desire did not extend to Nora. Anyone near merited her hatred. Nora went so far, after Robin left, as to try to "find" Robin by living her life, going to cafés, drinking with men, dancing with girls. She learned through these experiences that Robin was not only her lover; she was, as well, her daughter, for "Robin is incest too; that is one of her powers."[20] Nora picked up a French sailor, in her attempt to become "lost," but he took one look at the wooden horses in the bedroom and left. In the bedrooms of girls, she learned that she had been only an image to Robin rather than a person; a "fixed dismay" that only reminded Robin of her own distance from the human.

The doctor, now full of port and grief, staggers out and settles in the café he habituates. He is joined by an effeminate unfrocked priest. He pays no attention to the customers and waiters watching him as he declaims, for he now speaks out the fullness of his own misery. He has caught the contamination of other people's woe. He sees himself, for all his vicarious suffering, not as "a good man doing wrong, but the wrong man doing nothing much . . . ."[21] The doctor's condition degenerates rapidly. In a state of despair, he sees the futility of his own life and efforts; and he concludes the chapter saying "Now . . . the end—mark my words—now *nothing but wrath and weeping*!"[22]

While this final speech can be taken to mean that the doctor is destroyed, has come to madness, and foresees his own end, such a reading seems dubious at best. The doctor is dead drunk, and he has just come from a harrowing afternoon with Nora. At less maudlin moments, the doctor has more than once observed that suffering does not earn surcease from suffering. A man just continues to suffer until he dwindles into old age and finally death. The doctor will be sober, if still suffering, the next day. This speech is actually preparation for the last chapter; the doctor, as a kind of Tiresias, is foretelling of final calamity. He is suffering simultaneously for the past and the future. He identifies with both the pain Nora and Jenny have suffered and with the additional pain Nora will experience when she finally does find Robin. For it is Robin, not the doctor, who is hopelessly lost; and Robin is the focal figure of the novel.

VIII *"The Possessed"*

The final chapter of *Nightwood* is set in America. Jenny and Robin arrive in New York where they take a hotel room. Robin, who has changed drastically, seems "distracted"; she visits a good many churches but always in the attitude of a mourner. On one occasion, she lighted a candle before departing from a church; and Jenny, who had followed her, blew it out and relit it, as though to abort whatever prayer Robin may have made. Jenny, hysterical as a result of this change, suspects Robin of witchcraft; and her accusations only serve to drive Robin away.

Robin wanders into the country, where she seems to be trying to relate herself to something—anything—living. She pulls up flowers, and she seizes animals and draws back their fur to stare into their eyes. She is no longer of this world; her "engagements," we are told, are with "something unseen." She has ceased to function as an ego-conscious human. She takes to sleeping in the woods; and, when she finally comes to Nora's estate, she moves into a decayed chapel, and sleeps on a bench. When, one night, Nora's dog begins to bark, Nora unlocks the doors and windows as if she knows the barking may signal Robin's presence and as if she wants to make her home more accessible.

Nora follows the sounds of the dog until she sees a light in the chapel. When she enters the doorway, she discovers a makeshift altar which contains not only two lighted candles but flowers and toys, all placed before a Madonna. Robin is just about to kneel on the floor facing the dog who is between Robin and the altar. When the dog and Robin meet forehead to forehead, the dog springs backward whimpering; and Robin, now on all fours and "grinning and whimpering,"[23] pursues it. She backs the dog into a corner and strikes his side, and the dog snaps. It begins to bark, and Robin "in a fit of laughter, obscene and touching,"[24] also barks. Robin and the dog, now both crying, run together in circles until Robin "gives up;" she lies down, her arms out, and weeps. The dog also "gives up" and lies down, its head along her knees.

This scene depicts Robin's final attempt at communion with something living. Her grinning as she terrifies the dog may suggest her madness or her knowledge that what she is doing cannot work, that it is "obscene," or both. We are left with the characters in a tragic predicament. Robin and Nora are divided by an unbridgeable gulf: for one is beast; the other, human. But Robin's situation is the more tragic, for not only is she unable to reach across the isolation of her own now fallen nature to another human; she is also unable to reach backward to the purely animal nature to make contact. Robin ends frozen between the two worlds.[25]

IX *Structure in* Nightwood

A certain amount of critical "infighting" has become evident in discussions of *Nightwood*. The structure of the novel is of particular interest. In the initial experience of reading *Nightwood*, the first chapter and the first few pages of the second one present difficulties of orientation. We are plunged into a verbal "world," and we grasp for details with which to understand it. Shortly after these few pages in the second chapter, we begin to sense that our expectations of a linear and chronological presentation are being confounded. Instead of being told or shown "what happened," we discover we are lost in a welter of words and of passions having to do with events which have already occurred, or which have yet to happen. Or have they occurred? Where, that is, is the present in time? About whom or what is the novel constructed? Ultimately, we orient ourselves to "what happened" in some fashion which does not correspond to the words printed on the pages in consecutive order. We learn that we are viewing a particularly special kind of photograph album. It is a "family album" in which the members are related not by the immediate perceivable relationships of law and genetics; rather these family members are related by blood: the blood of humanity that antedates man's laws and customs. The album maker has chosen, moreover, to mount these photographs by memory association rather than by strict chronology. Thus some of the pictures, or what might better be called "tableaux," are clarified by others occurring either before or after the chronological event of reading the pages consecutively.

Joseph Frank in his article "Spatial Form in Modern Literature: Miss Barnes' *Nightwood*," calls this structure "spatial form." He distinguishes between two basic novelistic forms: the naturalistic and the spatial. A naturalistic novel progresses by a narrative time-sequence, and it depends for verisimilitude upon carefully delineated details which are "built-up" in accretions. But the spatially formed novel, even though it is necessarily read in a time-sequence, is an arrangement of images and details that are handled selectively. These details are of an imagistic or symbolic order, rather than being "real"; and they are intended to refer and reflect back and forth to one another. In *Nightwood*, the "real" world is not that important; the book exists for its own sake. To Frank, this kind of poetic imagery is Elizabethan since it attempts to fuse the "physical and psychological aspects of character . . . in an image or series of images."[26] *Nightwood*'s details have been selected, therefore, because of their symbolic significance rather than because of their lifelikeness. In fact, says Frank, *Nightwood* cannot be dealt with as a narrative structure. Rather, each chapter is like a searchlight "probing the darkness each from a different direction yet ultimately illuminating the same entanglement of the human spirit."[27]

To Walter Sutton in "The Literary Image and the Reader: A Consideration of the Theory of Spatial Form," the novel's "life" derives from an apprehension *in time* of words read in consecutive order. Both writer and reader join in this convention. But the image, which Frank defines as something that appeals to the senses, is to Sutton a "complex" both because of its associations with language and because each reader brings language associations of his own to the image-complex. Rather than being fixed in the reader's mind, the image-complex is subject to revision as the reading experience progresses. Thus Sutton regards even the structure of *Nightwood* as "not absolutely fixed in a spatial revelation or epiphany, but . . . organically flexible and adaptable, accommodating itself to every altered perspective in time."[28] The reader brings to the novel his own "historical consciousness . . ."; that is, the reader at no time suspends judgment. Rather, he is constantly relating images to one another; and he is even bringing apparently unrelated images into "meaningful configurations" by this kind of consciousness.

Sutton rejects the concept that Frank presents of images and phrases existing in *Nightwood* "independently of any time sequence." For Sutton observes that the "world" of the novel is very specifically placed in space and time. The events occur not anywhere and anytime but very precisely in "the cosmopolitan world of displaced Europeans and expatriated Americans in the post–World-War I years . . . ."[29]

In a dissertation on "The Orchestrated Novel,"[30] which defines that term and traces the impact of James Joyce upon Hermann Broch and Djuna Barnes, Jack Hirschman presents another structural possibility. The orchestrated novel is still defined as a poetic novelistic form, but such a novel shares with music certain characteristics which predominate over the linear or chronologically narrative forms of fiction. Three primary characteristics are noted: the use of verbal "leitmotifs" as a substitute for realistic or naturalistic detail as a means for imagistically creating characters and events; an abandonment of time-sequence as a method of story telling in preference for some form of organic, symbolic, or "synthetic" structure; and a conscious or even self-conscious preoccupation with language. James Joyce is cited as having been so preoccupied, especially in *Ulysses* and *Finnegan's Wake.*

To Hirschman, *Nightwood* resembles in structure a five-act play with traditional exposition, development, climax, denouement. At any given moment in which a character is dominant he is thought of as being "on-stage," and the rest of the characters are held in abeyance, "in the wings," as it were. Musically, *Nightwood* resembles a dramatic fugue, says Hirschman. The first four chapters introduce the characters, each in turn; chapters five through seven are episodes; and the final chapter is a coda. *Nightwood is* "contrapuntal in nature."

The term "orchestrated" seems more valid than the rather more specialized term "fugue." The structural problem of describing *Nightwood* is simply that fortuitous parallels of these kinds can be found in almost any novel. Hirschman is more accurate when he calls *Nightwood* "a poetic novel" since the adjective "poetic" does not limit our conception to a single organic form. "Poetic" does not specify that the novel *is* poetry; nor does "poetic" suppose that the use of metaphorical language is an end in itself. All structural interpretations of *Nightwood* suffer from the single failing of describing the skeleton of the work as though that were the entire body, flesh and all. While the term "poetic" is better than most, simply because it is less restrictive, it too is limiting; for it suggests that the novel was written principally for the sake of its language. What we are confronted with in Miss Barnes's best writing in *Nightwood*, can be described as *apprehended* tableau. The tableau, far more complex than the image, is pictorial (as most literary images are), but it is a composition very much like that of a painting. Robin is no more than a beautiful but lifeless image when first seen, for she is stretched out unconscious on her bed like a ballet dancer frozen in midstep. But that scene is far more charged with meaning than such an image implies since Felix is watching from behind a potted palm. The doctor, in a frenzy of fear that he may be apprehended for the illegal practice of medicine, is trying to help Robin without actually touching her. He is also much interested in her makeup table and in a hundred franc note lying in sight. The bellboy in his uniform is standing about, and behind Robin is the jungle of birds and plants she has created around herself. This highly charged composition is a tableau, not an image; the lifelessness of Robin is balanced against the energetic gyrations of the doctor who has a small "stage area" in which to move. The bellboy is the "witness" that the doctor must hoodwink to steal the money; his presence is necessary and forms an unspoken interaction with the doctor. Felix is the center of consciousness of the episode, for the reader sees all through his eyes.

But the reader does not really see or understand what Felix does, and for this reason the word "apprehended" must be prefixed to the term "tableau." For a proper understanding of that scene is not possible until much later in the book. In order to *apprehend* the tableau, the reader must grasp Felix's fictionalized history, his hopes for a family and a place in history, and his final acceptance of the terms of his own life while watching the disintegration of both his own and his son's lives. This tableau—Robin, the neglected birds and plants; the bellboy shuffling, waiting; and the doctor making "magic" with Robin's money and her vanity case—is truly a picture of calamity. Stated simply, we see this tableau twice: once on the printed page and once in an afterimage which provides the true perspective because necessary information is later supplied. In some cases, details are added later that must be placed within the initial scene in order to correct our apprehension of the tableau.

For example, we may use as illustration of this technique the doctor's introduction of Jenny to Robin as he reports it to Nora in the chapter "Watchman, What of the Night?" The true apprehension of this tableau depends upon the reader's knowing (though he has not yet been told) that Jenny already knew Robin a year before the doctor thought he had just introduced them. This knowledge, withheld for a time, changes the entire meaning of the scene that the doctor describes, as well as its implications. Instead of the major role he reports himself as having played, he is actually a pawn, the victim of a dramatic irony of which he knows nothing. Unless we visualize the introduction of the two women as the opera ends—both as described by the doctor (an admitted liar, since he admits also that he is describing Jenny as dressed in clothes she wore on another occasion) and as it really is—the truth behind the tableau does not emerge. The doctor is "used" in a social encounter which provides Jenny with the leverage to instigate her own purposes. Having known Robin for a year, she knows that Robin lives with Nora; and this relationship makes Robin valuable to Jenny—but not intrinsically valuable. Robin enjoys someone's love, and Jenny desires to steal something—this time something big; thus she covets the love between Nora and Robin. The point, then, is that the introduction of Robin to Jenny by the doctor is not what he reports it to be; it is actually the introduction of a mindless, willless human being, Robin, to the calculating Jenny, who wants Robin precisely because she "belongs" to someone else. Jenny is never really boosted up to the "banquet table of life," as the doctor thought; for, as defined in the novel, her major shortcoming is her inability to taste anything at all. Nora undergoes real suffering in her loss of Robin, but Jenny merely uses Robin's loss as a means for another secondhand experience—she tries to inflict pain upon Felix and his son in a later encounter.

A novel is an extended fictional work that tells some kind of story. For that story to be grasped, both the novelist and the reader must at some point come to terms with "what happened." Very simply, this means that a sequence of events has finally to be understood. The order of the telling is variable, for even the rather rigid narrative-sequence novel uses flashback and dream techniques which have the effect of casting the events backward or forward in time, or even of suggesting other forms of consciousness than the waking ego-dominant one.

When compared to other novels using flashback and other time-change techniques, the "structure" of *Nightwood* is really not that irregular. It begins in time with the earliest events occurring in the first chapter. Robin is introduced in the second chapter; she comes to know Felix and marries him. She has a child by Felix and then leaves him. In the third chapter, she takes up with Nora; in the fourth, she leaves her for Jenny. The bewildered Nora learns in the fifth chapter Dr. O'Connor's interpretation of the meaning of the night. In the sixth chapter, ten years after Guido's birth, Felix takes leave of Paris, the doctor, and the novel itself, as he moves to Vienna. In the seventh chapter, a final interview between Nora and the doctor makes it clear that Nora cannot (or perhaps will not) forget Robin; and the doctor leaves the novel screaming prophetically. The final confrontation between Robin and Nora's dog, with Nora as witness, is the latest event in the time of the novel; and it occurs in the final paragraphs. True, there are many time references to the past and some to the future in various chapters; but such time alterations are neither new, strange, nor unusual since they occur in many novels.

X Nightwood's *Center of Focus*

Nightwood tells of human entrapment as the unforeseen result of the characters' involvements with one another as each pursues his own needs. The theme is tragic because such characters are never able to relinquish their own desires to the needs of others. Because of their sexual natures, the characters are incomplete; and their sexual encounters only provide a temporary sense of wholeness. When the sexual rapport has ended, they are not only again alone but, even worse, are more acutely aware of their aloneness. The tragedy, then, consists not in the inevitability of death but in human experience itself.

Robin demonstrates this solitary condition to a radical degree, for her interaction with the other characters—such as Felix, Nora, and

Jenny—enforces the sense of estrangement. To speak of Robin is to refer at once to the structure, the theme, the meaning, and the poetry of *Nightwood;* for the novel's design and its purpose are incorporated in her. Although Burke and others have called *Nightwood* a lesbian novel, this is not exactly true. The novel does portray lesbian relationships, and the genuine lesbian love between Nora and Robin. However, Robin is not so much homosexual as bisexual; and the novel demonstrates the failure of the characters, either heterosexual or homosexual, to surmount on any level their own walled-in sense of estrangement. Felix is probably less damaged than the other major characters, for his contact with Robin has been the most fruitful: at least he has Guido; he has someone to love. He is not alone in still another sense, for he also has the companionship of the sexless Frau Mann. Although their relationship is admittedly sterile, Felix is still functioning in the world. Felix's relative wholeness can be clarified by juxtaposing our final glimpse of Felix with that of the doctor. Both Felix and the doctor are last seen in cafés where both are drinking heavily. But the doctor, entirely alone, even amid a crowd, is brought to a state of despair. Felix, who is accompanied by Frau Mann and who is drunk and tipping the band to play for him, is ever solicitous of Guido's welfare. And a benefit can even be seen (and supported by a number of Barnes's stories) for the sterility of Felix, Frau Mann and Guido. At least they are not advancing the miseries they have experienced by thrusting them upon future generations.

Dr. O'Connor, who bears the double burden of character and chorus, is a center-of-consciousness character, much in the Jamesian usage; he is "moved about" to be the witness of various scenes which he later describes. But, even as the father-confessor and the advisor who takes in "the wash of the world," he is noncatalytic. Everyone listens to him, particularly Felix and Nora; but no changes are ever brought about by the doctor's advice. For example, Nora is advised to forget Robin, which she is unable to do; Felix is told to treat Guido the way Felix is already treating Guido; and Jenny, who already knows Robin, is introduced to Robin. All the doctor gets for his efforts are his pains. Tiresias-like, he is able to foresee the future; Tiresias-like, he cannot alter its course; but, unlike Tiresias, the Doctor suffers unconscionably. For his gift of insight, or foresight, is purchased by his own sympathetic nature.

The doctor is necessary to the narrative because in his noncatalytic position as "outsider" to the events of the novel, he can be given knowledge which the other characters cannot. Felix, Nora and Jenny have not lost their belief in the possibility of attaining a state in which one is neither lonely nor alienated, and it is because of this hopefulness that they interact with Robin in the ways they do. However, in order for the reader to attain an objective view of what is going on, the doctor is necessary because he has lost these expectations in his own life, and functions as an "outsider" to the lives of the characters (Felix, Nora and Jenny) who are emotionally involved with Robin.

Real life extends the *illusion* of reconciliation of the Self to others. As the doctor says, most people marry and so "solve" the problem by postponing it indefinitely. Probably in the least examined lives this blurring of identities, or merging of them works best. In such a case, self-need in the one partner matches self-need in the other sufficiently to promote a workable relationship, and a person's *essential* aloneness in such cases need not be sensed until the final hour.

Nightwood is not the doctor's story, although he tells a good deal of it. He is qualified by his eloquence and experiences to describe the underbelly of the night world. What is most misleading about the novel is the predominance of his dialogue; for its volume (in both senses of the word) seems at times to be carrying the tenor of the novel. But his speeches do not represent the same point of view as that of the omniscient authorial voice. The doctor is after all, a subjective narrator whose views of the problems of the night, of love and loss, of pain and loneliness, are based upon his own experiences. He feels, for example, wronged by nature; he wants to be a woman. But at no point do Nora and Jenny indicate that they feel wronged. Robin, who is indeed wronged (but not so much sexually—nature has wronged her by misplacing her in time), is, at best, only unconsciously aware of the fact.

In effect the doctor blurs the issues of the novel with his great voice. He is authorized to speak of suffering, and the quality of his suffering may well match or exceed that of the other characters. But his is the suffering of the invert who wishes to be of the opposite sex. Nora's and Felix's sufferings are rooted in love and its loss. The doctor's is a world of brief encounters that are impersonal and untouched by love. Robin shares certain characteristics with the doctor in this respect, for she is entirely promiscuous and is even unable to resist the desires of others to possess her. But, unlike the doctor, who is not attractive to others, Robin leaves behind her a wake of hurt people who have fallen in love with her and whom she forgets. In effect, the doctor's experiences with the night end where Robin's begin.

Joseph Frank regards Robin as having been created at the moment of her awakening; she is not a character (having no human nature) but a "creation" who has not "attained the level of the human."[31] But Robin is certainly both a character in the novel and a person with human characteristics that are difficult to ignore. She does (at times) respond to Nora's love, and she does check her impulse to dash her baby to the floor. She can be made to feel "dirty"; she is aware, if uninterested, of Felix's views about history; she does read and underscore passages in DeSade; and she has apparently read quite widely since she summons the histories of famous real and fictional women. What Robin has attained, or perhaps been born with, is a *kind* of consciousness unlike that of civilized man. Robin has human qualities that it makes no sense to deny; but she also has a stronger animal nature than civilized man (in whom it is partly effaced). She is both a woman and a nocturnal animal. As a woman she has a need to be cared for; as an animal, she has an irresistible impulse to wander, particularly at night.

The imagery associated with Robin's appearance, posture, gait, is that of a lioness. Her swinging hair is manelike, and she drags her trenchcoat behind her like a tail. Robin, as the doctor points out, returns to her "lair" with the coming of the dawn. And the final chapter is appropriately set at that time of night when lateness is just prior to earliness. Being without a will, Robin will go anywhere with anyone. She is human enough to acknowledge important ties with Nora (as when she tells Jenny she cannot hurt Nora), but she is willless enough to become Jenny's lover while still living with Nora. Yet she does not leave until Nora drives her away, and this act is the other side of the theft Jenny perpetrated. Her theft could not have had such far-reaching consequences had Nora been able to control the result of her own bitterness and her damaged self-esteem because of her failure to understand Robin. Frank makes the point that Robin differs from the other characters only in degree, for all are involved "in her desperate dualism"[32] between the animal and the intellectual dimensions of the human personality. And Frank's remark might well be enlarged to suggest that in life itself all men are involved in a tension between their human and "prehistoric" or animal natures.

Robin plays with toys, dresses in boys' trousers, and is innocent. The nightlife she enters into does not touch her. Such a life may seem degraded to Nora and even to the doctor, but to Robin the night is gay and happy and carefree. And the story we are concerned with in *Nightwood* is that of Robin to whom such characters as the doctor or Nora are but adjuncts. Herein lies the difference between *Nightwood* and other literature of the 1920s which dealt with a night world and which presented it as depraved and hellish—with the night life of the invert depicted as the most degraded of all. But in *Nightwood* this life is not presented as a *de facto* reality but as a perceived reality that evokes in each individual a subjective response.

XI *Descent*

The "descent" thesis, so often described in *Nightwood*, is not at all clear-cut. The theory of a "descent" rests upon the critic's estimation of himself in relationship to others and to the human condition. Insofar as he is able to view himself as exempt from the primal alienated condition, he is able to see the progress of the novel in terms of descent. Jenny has had four husbands before meeting Robin, and it is suggested that she worried all four of them into the grave. Is it then a "descent" when she turns to Robin, a being she cannot harm? The doctor, for example, sees Jenny as having risen, boosted up to the banquet table of life, in her meeting Robin. Or has Nora descended? At no time is Nora's love presented as anything but fine. If anything, Nora has risen somewhat by the end of the work. For, if she has not been able to surmount her love for Robin, she has at least been able to understand its quality and the hopelessness of her situation.

Although Nora is not given to making moral distinctions, she does involuntarily possess a kind of aristocratic quality that prevents her from identifying wholly with others. The bedraggled whore who evokes sympathetic response in Robin is to Nora a "filthy baggage." As these different reactions indicate, the descent concept is entirely relative. The same night world in which Nora sees degradation (as does the doctor) is liberating to Robin; and her experiences in it, promiscuous as they are, do not impinge upon her sense of her own innocence. It is Nora's condemnation of that life that causes Robin to charge Nora with making her feel "dirty." Ironically, this same aristocratic, "rooted" background of Nora's destroys not only the relationship between Nora and Robin but Robin herself. In slapping Robin awake, Nora sets off the first event in a sequence that finally brings Robin to the "distracted" condition in which she is truly lost, even to herself.

Although to Nora, Robin may represent a socially prohibited love, as well as incest, Nora never ceases to long for her love. Finally, for Nora, Robin becomes the extreme identification of the Self with the Self, through another since Nora's love increasingly becomes a device for keeping the memory of love alive; and this memory resides entirely within Nora. Robin becomes an "intaglio" in Nora's bloodstream. According to Sutton, Robin extends beyond the Wordsworthian idealization of the innocent child to signify "regression" from mature consciousness. But, when the term "regression" is used, it should be understood that Robin's is a parabolic curve: she is introduced as an evolving creature, as the beast becoming human. What happens is that Nora checks forever the possibility (never very strong) of Robin's reaching a fully conscious human state. After Robin is slapped awake, or into something akin to a "normal" sense of guilt and shame—after she has been made to feel "dirty"—Robin is sent on a journey into total alienation that truly can be considered a descent. The final codalike chapter shows its effects and that is all. The Robin we are shown, prior to this last chapter, is wandering at night from bar to bar, from person to person; and she is completely innocent of any wrongdoing or evil. Robin mocks Nora's type, as one of those who want to "save us." The actual descent of Robin is mercifully hidden from us until we see its shocking effects—Robin's final inability to relate to either the human or the bestial—in "The Possessed."

Robin must be allowed the same subjectivity of perception that we ourselves daily experience and out of which we make our judgments. The night world of Paris and Berlin is as real as the daylight world of those (or any other) cities, yet the daylight world is forever blinded to an objective appraisal of Robin's world. As a result, Robin becomes the antagonist to a set of responses which judge her by standards which to her have no meaning. This problem of interpretation can be clarified somewhat by a brief examination into Robin's world as seen by three other writers.

Robert McAlmon collected, in *Distinguished Air*, stories of the night life in Berlin during the 1920s which show a totally abandoned way of life. Yet despite his deliberately objective and unimpassioned presentation, McAlmon still reacted subjectively. What appeared to have one value to him may have (indeed, must have) had quite another to some of the regular devotees of the cafés he visited. In the story "Distinguished Air," he describes patrons of a "Queer" café, and among them is an elderly man who appeared on one occasion dressed "as a blond-haired doll."[33] His characters move through a miasma of drunkenness and cocaine. In "Miss Knight," a male homosexual "modeled on a well-known expatriate figure,"[34] somewhat resembles *Nightwood*'s Dr. O'Connor: " 'I'm so glad I'm a real man' she shrieked across the room or cafe every now and then to relieve the tension and *ennui* that might, and does, settle upon all atmospheres at times."[35] And Dr. O'Connor, who also favors blond wigs and shouting, at one time tries to distract Nora from her troubles by describing a conversation with other homosexuals in which his "voice cracked on the word 'difference,' soaring up divinely . . . . "[36]

Well known is Hemingway's scene, early in *The Sun Also Rises*, in which Brett Ashley arrives at a Paris Café in the company of a group of homosexual men, who later make a travesty of the "thrill" of dancing with the whore Georgette. But Jake Barnes, who does not like these people, evinces neither sympathy nor understanding for them. They are supposed, he remarks, to be "funny," to be laughed at. But all Jake does is leave in order to avoid the temptation to hit one of them. Jake Barnes' attitude is what drives the homosexuals of Radclyffe Hall's *The Well of Loneliness* to Parisian bars where they can be with others of their own kind. The heroine of this novel, Stephen Gordon, a reserved, refined, and intelligent lesbian, is horrified by the bar. There she encounters men and women who have lost all self-respect and who are sold the drugs of their release from reality (again, it is cocaine) by a rapacious and inexorable proprietor. Transvestites parade the gawdy jewelry of their costuming at the bar where they can vent their natures with one another. Because they were born with natures as involuntarily homosexual as others are involuntarily heterosexual, these people have been stripped of "social dignity." Stephen can barely manage when approached by a drug-destroyed youth who calls her "sister" to respond with "Mon frère." The night life Stephen saw in the Paris of the 1920s was "garish and tragic."[37]

While Dr. O'Connor describes the night world as "descent" (we recall his description of girls cursing their sex in *pissoirs*), that is certainly not the way the night appears to Robin, the protagonist of the novel. To Robin, the night is filled with people about whom she makes no moral judgments. She talks with them all, goes home with many of them, eagerly anticipates each night's forays into that bright world. When she encounters the aging, gray-haired, and drunken whore, Robin comforts the woman, gives her "permission" to drink, and demands from Nora money to give to this woman so that she might purchase some small measure of happiness or comfort. Robin moves through the night world not like a socially despised person, as in *The Sun Also Rises*, or like an ill-adjusted person, a degenerate, or lost soul, as in *The Well of Loneliness*, but as one comfortable in her element. The nightlife she experiences, however it may appear to the doctor or to Nora, is a place and time of gaiety, music, and singing, as well as the delights of drunkenness and the bed.

To approach *Nightwood* from a structural viewpoint or to regard it as a "poetic" novel, is at once helpful and limiting; for, in either case, we are viewing the work externally as a form, or as a succession of "devices." Robin is the *raison d'être* of *Nightwood;* she dictates its form and inspires it poetry. She is the central reality about which the artifices of character, place, and situation function as the canvas flats, the "props," and the supporting characters of a play. But it would be idle for us to define Robin. Just as she herself is a mass of contradictions, what she represents extends itself into the often contradictory physical and spiritual characteristics of mankind. She is both the "Soul" of *Nightwood* and the "Soul," naturalistically presented, of man.

Robin is the essence of Self, or the selfness of the Self, made incarnate. Man, naturalistically seen, is an animal; he has an (evolved) animal body but no "Soul" in the Platonic sense wherein it is traditionally conceived that individuals contain within them an essence of self that transcends mortality. That Platonic "Soul" is thought to live forever, and it forms the basis for the promise of eternal life upon which so many religions build their theological structures. But, if man is regarded naturalistically, that quality of "essence," or "soul," must die with the body. Hence Robin is also the promise of death; for that elusive but palpable *real* sense of self, will, after all, cease at the moment of death, together with all longing for it. Robin is "eaten death," according to the doctor; and his remark is reinforced by the aura of decay that emanates from Robin's skin when she is in her trancelike sleep. Her slow life burns coldly like that of fungi, an "earth flesh" suggestive of our mortality; for we are all dying from the moment of our birth.

But Robin is also myth-engendering. She is first introduced to *Nightwood*'s pages amid the jungle she has created in her hotel room, under whose profuse plants and birds she lies in a deep sleep. Felix, "out of delicacy," steps behind the palms while the doctor attends to Robin. Felix is thus placed where Acteon concealed himself to observe Diana, where the Elders observed Susanna, and where countless swains have observed and fallen in love with endless nymphs. For Felix must surely fall in love with Robin as he observes her. If man's true history is legendary, as the doctor insists, Robin embodies that legend; for she is a "carrier" of the primal origins that man has all but forgotten during the long civilizing process.

The most profound level of Barnes's writing in *Nightwood* is existential. The distrust of "essences," which are "thoughts," derives from the existentialist's observation that every man must exist first, as a palpable reality, before he can think anything at all. This observation can be carried back in time to the earliest man and woman who had the first abstract thoughts. Whenever that was, whoever they were, that man and woman had to exist before their thoughts could take form—hence the existentialist distrusts "thought," "essence," and even verbalizations. "Truth" cannot be accurately put into words or thoughts, for Truth exists as a reality before it becomes an abstraction, and it antedates the thoughts and words which try to describe it. The only valid kind of reality, then, is, like Robin's, the lived life. That is, the less living is abstracted upon—the less it is verbalized, the less it postulates an "essence" of itself—the more that life is real. Robin is a relatively "pure" demonstration of this kind of reality. This view of life puts a premium on the active and immediate engagement of the individual with both himself—as a real participant of life—and with the immediately external: whatever that individual is brought into contact with.

This method of describing Robin postulates above all her incarnate reality. In other words, Robin is best realized as the fictional counterpart of a real person,[38] rather than as a "creation"—out of the stuff of pure imagination—whose only reality exists in the words of a book. The tendency of the fabulist, unlike that of the naturalist, is to put flesh upon an abstraction and make it walk, talk, and think like a real person. The weakness of this creative technique is that such imaginative characters always behave according to the intentions of their creator; for they have been created to subserve his purpose. They perform their duties faithfully, if sometimes unconvincingly. The naturalist, on the other hand, "reports." His is the uneasy task of attempting to show what he can of the movements and motivations of actual people. His models are taken from life, and his method of reporting is usually detailed—he uses many specific instances to prove his verisimilitude.

The generation of *Nightwood* can be said to have begun with chance—the fortuitous presence in the author's world of a real life model for Robin. The first creative act was the selection of that character to embody the mysteries and beauties of the *demi-monde*. Having made that initial selection, it became apparent that a double-value system would necessarily be involved. There was, on one hand, the daylight world—the world of moral judgment, of progress, of civilization—out of which the events in the life of such a character would lend themselves to the "descent" evaluation. To such a character herself, however, descent would be meaningless; for the night world and its people exist as they have existed through the centuries. Their lives were still real in the Paris of the 1920s and 1930s, and Robin partakes most fully of the immediacy of that life precisely because her sense of consciousness does not impinge upon her spontaneity. The problem that remained for the author, having made that initial choice, was to attach to this "lost" or "free" individual a sampling of other characters, all of whom would experience the loss of whatever this primal character represented to each of them. The choices, either real or fictional, are logical enough: a husband, a son, two representative lesbian lovers. O'Connor was brought in from *Ryder* since the novel required an articulate spokesman to explain the night, and the necessity of the doctor's presence is readily apparent when we consider Barnes's characteristic tendency to maintain an artistic and objective "distance" from her subjects.

The author's presence lies behind the story in that inverted naturalism in which man is thought of as an evolved creature who lives under the sentence of death and in which that sentence constitutes his only solace. Because of her peculiar kind of consciousness, Robin is unaware of the determinism that is destroying her; the author, however, is aware of the determinism of events. It is thus possible for the descent thesis to be invalid because such a category is dependent upon the world of daylight values; but at the same time the determinism set in motion by Nora's slapping Robin destroys Robin's chances to be human—in effect it destroys her—but not for moral reasons. Rather the reverse, if anything, is the case; for, in making the moral judgment that Robin has "fallen," Nora harms Robin. Again, at the end of the novel the author's presence is apparent; for, in choosing such an ending, Barnes has rejected the logic of determinism which calls for death to end the human tragedy, just as she rejects the moral judgment which calls for a degraded or disgusting picture—the "consequences" of the morally illicit life. Rather, the author has chosen to "freeze" and so to immortalize Robin, Nora, and the dog. Just as Poe's raven *still* is sitting on the bust of Pallas over the student's door, so Robin, Nora, and the dog finally become a fixed dismay, a state of mind. What is condensed from both the Poe poem and from *Nightwood*, finally, is beauty: the memory of the beloved and beautiful woman hopelessly lost. A judgment, even a "moral" judgment, can be said to have been made by the author in so preserving Robin in that final tableau. In this naturalistic (if poetic) evocation of a real person, the author is evidently unwilling to show Robin as dead. And symbolically speaking, of course, Robin cannot be dead so long as what she represents remains alive.

Nightwood is a poetic novel that is naturalistic in its purpose. It does not, as Frank points out, create its characters by the accretion of lifelike details but by the poetic evocation of select and "telling" images. But this poetic technique in the evocation of Robin should not be thought to mean that Robin's creation depends upon the exclusion or withholding of details so as to engender artificially a sense of the mystery of Robin. All that has been withheld from the reader are the lyrics of the songs that Robin has picked up in bars, as well as mundane bits of dialogue. Robin talks but little, and her speech is not revealing. When she does speak, it is with her usual sardonic intonation; and her remarks concern only present events.

As a result, Robin *is* mysterious and elusive; she *is* unfathomable. What is given of Robin is all that is known—and is all that can be given. The details, few as they are, are poetically presented to show not as little but as much as can be shown. Robin has been "immortalized" in the pages of *Nightwood* by sheer force of will. To revert again to the fable as an analogy, the fabulist can get his characters to do whatever he plans for them to do; that is how they are designed from the start. But Robin cannot be made to do anything; she can barely be kept abreast of; we get glimpses of her, for that is all that can be hoped for. The author is thus the "reporter," who, scarcely better off than the reader, strives to record that which is all but untransferable from life to print. Herein lies the chief source of mischief for the readers, the reviewers, and the critics alike: reading *Nightwood* as "make believe," as surrealistic fantasy, or even as a poetic novel, tends to make it a "safe" book, one which does not threaten in any way the security of the reader. When *Nightwood* is approached as the author's struggle to capture that ineluctable, human nature-animal nature from which we derive(and to which we pay a thousand unconscious allegiances), the character of Robin leaps from the page to challenge our very life-style. Frozen, immortalized, in that final tableau are Robin, the dog, and Nora: three dimensions of the Self, each forever separated from the other.

CHAPTER 7

The Ultimate Synthesis: Poetry and Drama

MISS BARNES'S verse drama *The Antiphon* (1958) appeared twenty-two years after *Nightwood*. A warlike world forms the background of the play; the time of the action is 1939, when the Germans were bombarding England. The location, Burley Hall, is an ancestral home which had been a college for chantry priests a couple of centuries previously. The house is a visible symbol of the civilized past and its traditions. Since Burley is badly damaged—the doors and windows are gone from their frames; a wall has been blown down—the house is also a symbol of the destruction of the modern world. The condition of the house, with its contents, suggests, moreover, the divided and hostile condition of modern man. The individuals summoned to Burley not only are divided persons within themselves but they are also the exploded fragments of what had once been a family. Where once, with its walls, doors and windows intact, the house suggested the sanctity of private life, at present strangers on their way to port wander through the house and appear at times upon the upper balcony where they look down in idle curiosity upon the drama occurring below.

Prior to the beginning of the play, Jeremy, the youngest of three sons, has summoned to Burley Hall his mother Augusta, a woman of eighty; his two brothers, Dudley and Elisha; and Miranda, the only daughter, the eldest of the children (about fifty years old), and an actress and writer. The family has been divided for so long that its members have become, for the most part, strangers to one another. Jeremy disguised as "Jack Blow," a coachman, knows his sister, although she does not realize who he is; and Dudley, a manufacturer of watches, is in daily contact with his brother Elisha, his publicity agent. Jeremy's intentions in summoning together mother, daughter, and sons is to remedy the family estrangement. His choice of location is the house in which his mother was born and reared. Into that house he will convey in Act 2 a model of the American home in which Augusta lived after marrying—a replica of the birthplace of her children. Although the ancestral Burley is unknown to Dudley and Elisha, Miranda is familiar with it; for she has been using the hall as a storage place for costumes and other theatrical belongings.

The contents of this ruined home suggest more than Miranda's acting profession. There are, as well, relics of a former family life suggested in the chinaware, the toys, and the musical instruments. Other objects lying about suggest that the family's history is that of mankind. In view are a heavy curfew bell (perhaps from the days when priests lived there), a dummy in a British soldier's garb (suggestive of man's warlike history), and battered statues. Visible beyond the house are the remains of a wall and what had once been a colonnade, and these seem "wasteland" artifacts, much in the manner they are imaged in the T. S. Eliot poem.

Jeremy, for reasons never explained, chooses to remain disguised to his family, although the reader is soon made aware of his identity. Jonathan Burley, Augusta's aged brother and the caretaker of Burley Hall, addresses Jeremy by name in the closing moments of the play, suggesting that he has known from the start that "Jack Blow" is really Jeremy. A possible explanation for his disguise might suppose that the peacemaker must be neutral to the issues for which he seeks a reconciliation. Jeremy disguises himself as the Fool, in the Shakespearean sense; he is the Fool who speaks too wisely, if obliquely; and his comments appear as non sequiturs to the other characters. While his role is usually passive as to involvement in the family matters that are discussed, Jeremy makes possible a sustained dramatic interest that is needed especially in the exposition of act 1.

The Antiphon is written in three one-scene acts. The action is continuous from act 1 to act 2; and the players assume, as the second act begins, the same positions they have at the end of act 1. A time lapse of an hour or so occurs between the second and third acts. A case can be made, as well, that act 3 actually consists of two scenes that run consecutively and without formal interruption.

I *Act 1*

The play begins with the arrival of Miranda and "Jack Blow," actually Jeremy, at Burley Hall. They find the building, devastated by recent bombing, to be empty, but they had expected others to be awaiting them. Jack makes an allusion to Miranda's acting talents by applauding her "entrance"; and throughout the drama, he is playful and seemingly inconsequential, while Miranda's attitude is somber. If this Miranda is named for Shakespeare's Miranda in *The Tempest*, she is much altered since she left the magic island of Prospero. From Miranda we learn that at Burley Hall her mother had imbibed her taste for the great names of royalty and legend, and also her yearning for a fame she had hoped to achieve by mothering greatness. Instead, she married Titus Higby Hobbs of Salem, an American, and gave birth to her own discontentment. The sons she favored disappointed her, and Augusta rejected her daughter and her accomplishments.

Titus had been, in his youth, a stylishly dressed ladies' man, a believer in polygamy, and a lover of an entire horde of women. He had come to England with his mother, Victoria, very much as had Wendell Ryder and Sophia in *Ryder*. Titus, like Wendell, was something of a musician and composer, for the family that *The Antiphon* dramatizes is essentially the one whose history is humorously recorded in *Ryder*.

Miranda is clearly afraid of her brothers, whose arrival she anticipates; and "Jack Blow" makes the thematic connection between Miranda's fears and the upsetting of all order which he foresees in the commencement of World War II. He prophesies, in fact, a future totalitarian world led by power-mad men who are not unlike the brothers Dudley and Elisha who will end by destroying civilization because of their own gluttony. In a soliloquy, Jack compares himself with Esau; he observes that all men betray themselves; but he regards his outcast state as kingly. Ominous and threatening is the initial appearance of Dudley and Elisha, who conceal themselves to observe Jack and the aged caretaker, Jonathan Burley. Yet when Jack and Jonathan depart, the brothers' entrance loses its sinister quality. Symbolic, even Absurdist, technique quickly replaces the almost Jacobean threat when Dudley—watch in hand, and grasping his open umbrella—enters through a window. Elisha, younger and more stylish, characteristically eats almonds and tosses the shells about. The two brothers suggest, visually, a time-ridden, wasteful self-indulgence. On the one hand, Dudley is cautious and conservative (his open umbrella suggests the unreality for him of all that Burley stands for); on the other hand, Elisha is evocative of a fashion-conscious and wasteful consumerism. The American way of life with its preoccupations with time, money, and power sustains in the two brothers Miss Barnes's most severe indictment.

Dudley and Elisha have never seen their mother's birthplace, nor do they understand the artifacts of their own civilization: the objects and furnishings lying about them. Their ignorance causes them to react violently to these objects. The ominous fact gradually disclosed is that the two have conceived of this summons to Burley as an unusual opportunity for themselves. They are impatient about Augusta's tenacity to life, and they have come to Burley with the idea of hurrying their mother into her grave. The opportunity is right, Dudley assures Elisha; and the upset of war will conceal their deed. Besides, since Augusta is very old, her death would surprise no one.

But why do these men seek their own mother's death? Here are men of wealth and position. Simple greed cannot be the motive. Dudley has a thousand and more employees over whom he can lord it; yet only by attacking the roots of his own existence can he hope to rise to a sense of autonomous selfhood. Only by destroying his own inheritance can man stand amid the ruins he has made and proclaim himself to be his own creator. His intentions are based upon immaturity, childishness, and (growing out of these) spite, hatred, and envy of the truly adult. When his sister is unexpectedly present, Dudley extends his destructive intentions to include the equally despised Miranda; he proposes a double murder.

The conspirators, Dudley and Elisha, again conceal themselves when Jack returns with Burley. By now thoroughly curious, Jonathan demands that Jack identify himself. There follows a riddling speech—one comic and veiled behind Jeremy's denomination of himself as "Tom-O'Bedlam" and "Latern Jack"—as he sustains his Fool's disguise while recounting how he and Miranda fled Paris. Acting as if Jonathan does not know his own niece, Jack explains that Miranda is an actress, a member of the Odéon Theater, who has played the Comédie-Française. Now, he says, they are taking a ship in the morning, evidently for America. Jack says he met Miranda in Paris, but he has apparently been "shadowing" her for years, anonymously looking after her, and taking bit parts in some of her productions. He was, he mentions, a spear carrier in one of her plays.

Jonathan concludes that, since Jack looks after Miranda, he will therefore "betray" her. Jeremy's reply that she will "undo herself" is prophetic. She has a royal bearing but is a "bumpkin"; she is bold enough but essentially helpless. Jeremy's description of his sister forms a dramatic anticipation to the climax of the play when Miranda and Augusta, each imaged in the other, will undo themselves. Jeremy's "Therefore, let us begin it"[1] suggests not only the inevitability of Miranda's undoing but also that the first act has been the prologue to the action of the play; for, as the act ends, Miranda appears on the upper balcony, and Dudley and Elisha make their presence known. As the curtain closes, the tapping of a cane is heard as Augusta approaches Burley, and Miranda's protesting "No, no, no, no, no, no!" forms the dramatic but mysterious climax to this act.

II *Act 2*

The first-act action of *The Antiphon* leads directly to that of act 2. Dudley is sitting at the head of the table; his hat is on, and his open umbrella is still upraised. Elisha, leaning against the dressmaker's dummy, continues to crack almonds and to scatter the shells. Both brothers are positioned to cast an ironic light upon their life roles and their family relationships. Miranda remains on the balcony. Augusta, old and gaunt, is dressed in severe black, even to her flat-crowned hat. Having been summoned to her father's house by Jeremy, she demands to know where he is. She recognizes Dudley and Elisha, as well as her daughter, but without enthusiasm. She does not know Jeremy nor, until he identifies himself, her brother Jonathan.

Augusta is an acerbic, talkative, and disappointed woman. Her arrival can be said to complete this family reunion, but ironically; for, as soon as they are gathered, they begin to renew their old hostilities. The aged Jonathan is proud of his niece Miranda; she has made a name for herself as an actress in France and as a writer in England. Dudley will hear no praise of his sister; to him she may have some slight credit in Beewick (the location of Burley Hall), but she would be unknown in New York. Augusta is tartly critical of Miranda's dress, for she does not understand that Miranda fled Paris still wearing the costume of her latest stage performance. Miranda, garbed in velvet and wearing an elaborate feathered hat, is "dressed," Augusta says, "as though there were no God."[2]

Augusta, who is so critical of her daughter, not only admires Miranda's rings, but also asks for them. Miranda gives her mother the rings, and thus begins the transfer of costume which is completed early in act 3. As mother and daughter intermix possessions and identities, each is on the way to becoming the objectified Self of the other.

The brothers' comments about Miranda reflect more about themselves than their sister. Elisha scorns her as a "Duchess," an evident aspersion of Miranda's dignified carriage. To Dudley, however, Miranda is "Queen of the Night," a remark that implies possibly a disreputable life, or possibly that Miranda is being referred to as an author who has written something like *Nightwood* that expresses knowledge of or intimacy with the night. Augusta's remarks partake of the same flavor; Miranda is too "ambiguous." However Augusta frankly prefers sons; and her deprecatory attitude toward women is expressed when she asks "What's a woman?" When Dudley replies to her with the definition, "a cow, sitting on a crumpled grin,"[3] he indicates that Augusta cannot really turn to her sons; for, like Dudley, they parry her throughout.

The family spite turns to its original source, Titus, who estranged himself from society with his espousal of polygamy, free love, and "free everything." Titus, who brought Augusta to America, went from New York to Pendry Cove to Spuyten Duyvil, and, finally, to "Hobbs Ark," his home. Like Wendell Ryder, he built his own home but did not farm the land. "Hobbs Ark" is, of course, *Ryder's* "Bulls-Ease"; but the home is now regarded by those who have returned with a perspective influenced by time and distance. Dudley and Elisha reconstruct from memory of Titus's women a typical scene in which Augusta would be scrubbing the floors while Titus's women sat drinking coffee and while Titus's mother Victoria knitted. Titus himself, meanwhile, would most likely be reading his Bible to find passages that would affirm his opinion of himself as a great father figure.

The catalogue of Titus's women contains so many that even his family quarrel about their very identities. Jonathan points out that Titus began his "practice" in Beewick with a woman who dressed entirely in red. But Dudley confuses this woman with "Louise," and

Elisha complicates the discussion by supposing that they are really speaking of a girl Titus found on a Lake Erie barge. This comedy of cross-purposes over nothing is increased by Augusta who corrects everybody: they are confusing the red-clothed woman with Belinda. They refer, she insists, to Juliette of Camberwell; and Dudley admits he was thinking of Kitty Partingale, who played the harp. Miranda, drawn by now into this discussion, recalls Kitty as a clairvoyant; and Augusta is suddenly reminded of Trudy Frisch, who apparently left Titus.

Titus's mother Victoria, like Wendell's mother Sophia, kept a salon and was a compelling woman. Both mothers clearly influenced their sons with their own liberated social attitudes; both were in love with knowledge, but were "faulty" scholars; both were twice married; and both were abandoned by their second husbands for strumpets. Married life for Augusta, forty years later, is viewed with bitterness; for she thinks she married Titus because of her romantic "storybook" attitudes as a young woman. She was apparently able to reconcile herself to Titus's sexual principles by convincing herself that, since he would truly father greatness, she would achieve that nearness to rank and fame she longed for through her children. Her hope was in the sons she would have, but they disappointed her by preferring money to greatness. And, because of her disposition to deprecate women, she can see no credit to herself in Miranda who is, after all, only another self to Augusta.

The instant Jack and Burley leave to carry in the doll's house, the two brothers, now alone with Augusta and Miranda, physically attack them. Dudley dons a pig's mask, and Elisha an ass's. Elisha, striking away Miranda's cane, pins her arms behind her, manhandles her, kicks at her, and subjects her to a vilification that reflects his and Dudley's lifelong resentment of their sister and all she represents. She is accused for her spinsterhood and for trying to live up to Titus's "Grand Conception," which is essentially the hedonistic "Credo" Wendell followed in *Ryder*. She is accused of drunkenness; and Elisha rudely proposes a rape and ends by tripping her. Miranda, who retaliates within the limits of her own dignity, will not abandon herself or her ways to achieve the "slum" of her brothers' good opinion. The pig's head unmasks the avaricious Dudley, and the ass's mask does the braying of the publicity agent Elisha. The brothers' attempt on these women's lives is tempered by their own lack of strength and resolution. Dudley makes use of

Jeremy's carriage whip to make Augusta dance; but, as Augusta declares, she is a "cold mouse" at eighty and cannot. Augusta is so mistaken about her sons' intentions that she believes they are playing with her.

This macabre scene of horror ends as abruptly as it began. The brothers unmask when Jeremy and Jonathan carry in the doll's house replica of "Hobb's Ark." Augusta is lifted to the table where she sits before the house and draws forth a stick with dolls attached who represent Titus's mistresses. When she opens the roof, another doll pops out that represents Titus. In a scene reminiscent of Hamlet's conversation with the skull of Yorick, she addresses this doll; but Hamlet's "where be your gibes now?"[4] is replaced by Augusta's curiosity about the diminution to the sliver of a mere stick of Titus's "stallion yard" of which he was so proud. Augusta answers her own question about how "Jack Blow" could build the replica by assuming that he has been told everything about the family by Miranda. Her answer is incorrect, for it is completely out of character for Miranda to reveal anything at all.

The tale of this family's history now plunges into the regions of Oedipal sublimation and of the Electra complex. For, as Augusta peers into a replica of her daughter's bedroom, she recoils from the memory of the day that may have transformed Miranda's entire personality. Miranda herself relates the scene when, sixteen years old, she submitted to rape by an Englishman who was three times her age. As part of the principles of his "credo," Titus had urged his daughter to the deed; and Augusta, who knew what was happening, had done nothing to prevent it.

Earlier, Dudley had alluded to Miranda's childhood relationship to her mother as having been built upon guilt. There had been a great many whippings, and Miranda had come to welcome them and to furnish her mother with the means to give her her own masochistic punishment. Just as Miranda had submitted to her mother's whippings as atonement for the puritanic and senseless guilt feelings instilled in her, she submitted, like a sacrifice, to her father's wishes. What is not suggested here, but is revealed in act 3 in a carefully veiled speech by Miranda, is that a strong incestuous undercurrent existed between the father and the daughter. But the consummation had to be effected by a third party acting as surrogate.

Act 2 ends as the family goes in to dinner, quite as though nothing had happened. Miranda, alone with her uncle, requests that he not be present for what is to follow, for she foresees tragic consequences to this reunion.

III *Act 3*

After dinner, Miranda is sleeping on the circus griffin, the two halves of which have now been brought together to form a bed; and lace curtains shroud the bed tent-fashion. The "boys," as Augusta calls them, are presumed to be asleep in the upper gallery. Actually, however, they are very much awake; and they trigger by their departure the tragic events that end the play. When Augusta climbs upon the griffin, she evinces a playful mood which takes years away from her and causes her to behave as if she were a girl again. She wants to play. The "epilogue," she says, is over, suggesting that the first two acts have constituted the "real" play. For the "boys" are in bed, just as in the early days of her motherhood; and it is time for make-believe. But, if the play is over, there is a double entendre use made of the word "play"; for Augusta wants to play now, in the sense of sport; and the real play, the drama of the "antiphon" is about to begin.

Miranda is not in a mood for play. Futile as her quarrel with her mother is, she cannot stop it; and, when Augusta would pretend that the griffin upon which both are now mounted can carry them away to imagined places, Miranda resists. She blames her mother for having conceived her; she regards herself as victim of her parents' passions; and, because she was created, she must suffer the pain of death. Bitter that she was born at all, Miranda sees conception as death and, even worse, as murder. Augusta's recourse to the childhood world of fantasy and make-believe seems to be her answer to the realities Miranda presses upon her. Augusta imagines herself to be an empress; a singer of fame; a legendary "sea-hag"; and the Sleeping Beauty. Still, disillusionment and disappointment inform much of her speech; she would like something to make her life meaningful. Her search for her own significance, combined with her tendency to see herself in her daughter, provoke her to demand more closely of Miranda who or what she is. But Miranda's only remark is that she lives by a "hard-won" silence; she has elected a monastic existence; and she will have nothing to do with the world and its ways.

A kind of hermaphroditic image, "My daughter is winged serpent, *and* the urn,"[5] suggests that, to Augusta's sensibilities (really not that different from those of Dudley and Elisha), Miranda has in some way denied nature—or has perhaps embraced it too wholly by taking both male and female natures to herself. She presses upon Miranda the rumor of her forty lovers, which Miranda angrily refuses either to confirm or deny; for Miranda will have no part of worldly gossip. Augusta tries to weep in order to touch her daughter, but she admits she has no tears because she has "grinned" them all away in a vain effort to please her sons. Miranda herself speculates about the relationship between Oedipus and his mother, and she wonders what he saw after he blinded himself.

In rapid succession Augusta inquires of Miranda who "Sylvia" was: whether a woman was indeed so loved that she could lie peacefully in death "beneath a ton"; whether, finally, a legendary mermaid truly did emerge from the sea to take a lover. These mysterious questions that seem out of context, make some sense if Miranda is regarded as a persona for the author herself, for there is the little girl Sylvia of *Nightwood*, and there is the poem "Crystals" that describes a king's daughter who is lying "Wax-heavy" in her tomb.[6] The final question about the mermaid seems to refer directly to the fisherman-mermaid legend which formed the basis for the one-act comedy "Kurzy of the Sea."

Augusta reverts to the family's violent and public end when Titus, capitulating to the law's demand that he lead a monogamous life, abandoned his family for one of his mistresses in order to make his life "respectable." Miranda is still puzzled by her father's collapse after he had for so long presented himself as a man of strength. For out of fear he denied the "called response." Miranda's puzzlement evokes the title of the play, for the "called response," the antiphon, underscores the tough morality or sense of responsibility to self that the play urges. Miranda is not calling into question the absolute rightness or wrongness of Titus's views of life; rather, she seems to insist upon a notion of justice to self and to others which fails when a person denies his convictions.

Augusta insists that every woman keeps a "battlement" in her heart to resist her husband. Miranda was born into this "lost equation" as if to "mend" the economy. The suggestion persists that Miranda would have transformed herself into her mother had she been able, but this incestuous alternative was not possible for her. Again, Barnes suggests sublimated incest between father and daughter. Mother and daughter are by now in completely exchanged costumes; for Augusta now has the hats, boots, cloak and rings of Miranda. Thus, as the two women begin circling each other in mounting hostility, each becomes symbolically the other's lost identity.

Augusta still demands of her daughter that she rectify Augusta's life: "*Make me something!*" she demands. Miranda points out that both her mother in her generation and Miranda in hers are beset by discontentment and that both must accept their estrangement as a kind of bond. By now mother and daughter are at the foot of the stairs, Miranda is fending off her mother with her skirts outspread, and Augusta is "following" (not pursuing, though the situation is ambiguous). Since Augusta is so identified with Miranda and is by now wearing her clothes, Augusta confusedly becomes Miranda chasing Augusta; each is pursuing and following, simultaneously, the other. When Miranda points out that Augusta's is a "key -gone" generation, the musical figures of her speech refer to a generation which has lost the "key" to meaning; and, as a result, its random sounds have dissipated themselves into the air. Because mother and daughter have exchanged identities, Miranda is also accusing her own generation; but she tries to be objective and philosophical. Augusta, who characteristically takes Miranda's remarks personally, thinks her daughter means that because of her advanced age Augusta will soon die. When Augusta retaliates that a grave awaits Miranda as surely as for herself, the grave is hardly a threat to Miranda; for death is the "rate" by which she measures all she does.

During these exchanges, the two women have been steadily ascending the staircase; and Miranda is in the higher position. As they approach the top landing, Miranda tries to stop Augusta, in order to prevent her mother's reaching her brothers who, as she vainly attempts to explain because of a previous incident, have murderous intentions. At this moment, the brothers are heard fleeing and, when the mother and the sister descend by the other staircase, Miranda is still in front and is seemingly in the way to prevent Augusta from reaching her sons. The entire figure of the rise and descent suggests that Augusta has always blamed her daughter (but as alter ego, really herself) for coming between her and her sons. Augusta cannot accept the outright reality that the brothers care nothing for her and are in fact moral reprobates. Miranda, caught between her mother and her brothers, must necessarily see herself as the "victim" who catches blame for everything and who is always serving as a helpless buffer between bewildering and bewildered forces.

When Augusta commands Miranda to get out of her way, Miranda responds by asking her mother to abandon her sons just as they have abandoned her. When a sudden, "derisive" blast of the car horn signals the departure of the brothers, the women have reached the foot of the stairs; and Augusta, transported by her loss of her sons, begins ringing the heavy bell as she waves it threateningly at Miranda. She charges Miranda with her sons' departure, with her own impending death, even with her old age, and with her sense that all is lost. The climactic moment of the play occurs as Augusta brings the bell down upon Miranda's head; and as both fall across the griffin, they pull down the curtains and heavy ornate crown upon themselves. The two women have died in a love-death embrace of misapprehensions; nevertheless, their dying may be the true antiphon of the play. Death, it is suggested, is not the calamity; life is.

Jonathan appears on the balcony; and Jeremy, who reenters, blames himself for having vainly attempted to mend his family's troubles. But Jeremy knows that all has been lost from the beginning: "This is the hour of the uncreate;/The season of the sorrowless lamenting."[7] Jack appears indifferent as he leaves the stage and ends the play.

IV The Antiphon's *Indictment*

In *Hamlet*, the people were "muddied" by internal corruption; something was "rotten" in Denmark. Whether or not Shakespeare was actually referring to contemporary England, the issue was national; hence, localized. However corrupt Shakespeare's world may have been, it was still the Renaissance world that had a great deal of creative energy and that was expansive and adventurous. *The Antiphon* presents a much more sweeping indictment than did *Hamlet*. Born of nineteenth-century pessimism and the industrial revolution (among other forces), both material and philosophical tendencies conjoin to produce a twentieth century of disillusionment, despair, and large-scale violence. *The Antiphon* builds upon that now universal condition. For all real purposes, the civilized world of Western man has already died when this play begins. No hope is possible. Even looking backward (which is suggested by the use of the doll's house replica in act 2), rather than permitting a fresh start, only intensifies the recriminations. The past merely affirms that the seeds of destruction were present from the beginning. Who is to blame? Everyone, evidently; yet no one accepts either his own guilt or his responsibility. Miranda, then, voices the play's dark theme: to have been born at all is a disaster. Conception is murder, and all men stand condemned. The human race is grasping, power mad, and status seeking.

Even the artist, represented by Miranda, is shown to be caught in human ugliness and to be swept, willy-nilly, to destruction. Man has been so unsuccessful in managing both himself and his world that the only cure (which a number of Barnes's stories has shown to be an impossibility) is an end to all procreation. Miranda's personal code of behavior is "noble"; she accepts blame and responsibility; she urges the perspective of objectivity concerning human affairs and humanistic dealings with all people; and she counsels a stoic resignation in facing death. Her urgings have no power, however (any more than Matthew O'Connor's "advice" to friends in *Nightwood*), to deflect the course events take. The artist may be the best the human race has devised, but the artist's productions are exercises in futility. He or she has been stripped of important motivation to "communicate." More than ever before—more than in *Ryder* and much more than in *Nightwood*—the audience to which *The Antiphon* is directed has been narrowed since it no longer matters whether the human race can understand its artists; the destruction is complete. Hence *The Antiphon*, beyond either hope or despair, must exist for its own sake.

V *Imagism and* The Antiphon

The Antiphon is the culmination of the tendencies, techniques, and knowledge that extend back to the beginnings of Miss Barnes's writing career. Her earliest work, *The Book of Repulsive Women* (1915), as well as other early poetry, had etched its figures in the sharp, clean lines of the Imagist. Nothing wasted, nothing "meant," the poems *are* what they mean. Richard Aldington had set forth Imagism's tenets in the *Little Review:* the subject was to be treated directly and without emotional involvement or comment. Rather than "tell" the reader of an emotion, for example, the image was to carry that burden. Another point had to do with the nature of the image: it was to have "hardness" or clarity; rather than appeal to sentiment the image was to be more objectively visual. The Imagist sought, as well, to create innovative rhythms and to avoid traditional forms. Finally, Aldington stressed the importance of choosing the accurate word to convey exactly what was intended. The Imagists, above all, were breaking away from any fuzziness of meaning or intent.[8]

An early Barnes poem, "Antique," illustrates the poet's grasp of these concepts. The poem is a portrait in three stanzas of a woman's head. She wears a linen hood; she has a lace ruff into which is fixed a cameo; and her hair, a shining amber, is braided about her head. Her lips are thin, and they shape an "oddly wise" mouth. Her nose, also thin, is Greek. The final and telling image is that of the whole face:"A profile like a dagger lain/ Between the hair"[9] Since "Antique" is a word with a strong, positive connotation for Barnes, the lady described need not be old; indeed, she is probably young. She is presented as unique, as a worthy poetic subject; for she does not live either in or for the present time.

Her "oddly wise" mouth negates the innocence of absolute youth, however; and her Greek nose invokes a culture as old as the beginnings of Western civilization. She wears a cameo—a piece of jewelry often prized as an antique and one frequently handed down through the generations within a family—and even the lace ruff and linen cowl do not bespeak the twentieth century. The woman's mouth must suggest that she lives in her own time: that she knows enough of life to have become detached from the momentary. The profile, "like a dagger," is itself a cameo; and the hair forms a "ground" or frame. A sharply chiseled profile, like those seen on cameos, it emphasizes a classic economy comparable to that of the silhouette. We see only what is important: the clean lines of a just proportion. The "muted" eyes suggest that outward seeing is not emphasized in the person who lives outside of time. We see, then, how Barnes's short poem can reach beyond the fashion, the fad, and the moment to limn a face worthy of the artist's admiration.

In *Ryder*, Miss Barnes's interest in and use of language reached back as far as the Bible and, in an often dazzling display of virtuosity, progressed through Chaucer, Milton, Fielding, and the Elizabethans. In *Nightwood*, a poetic, imagist voice was successfully fused with the prose form of the novel; but a metamorphosis (created perhaps by the demands of the novel) transformed the simple image into a living tableau, or "image complex," that is subject to time, to movement, and to a doubly subjective condition. Each character speaks, describes, and creates images out of his own subjectivity; and the reader reaches out of his own subjective perceptions of the book and reassembles those changing image-impressions for himself. Finally, a modern diction is used.

Miss Barnes's choice of the dramatic form for *The Antiphon* cleared the way for a truly poetic language by entirely freeing her from the descriptive part of narration. In drama, the actors in their costumes and on their set *are* the images themselves. Once established, they can be seen in production or visualized in a reading. The dramatic form allows for a true exploration of poetic language as characters reveal their thoughts, but all descriptions would necessarily be of the past or future, since all that occurs on the stage is in the present and can be seen. The dialogue is spoken by separate individuals, and each perceives subjectively both the present and the past (and, in the case of Jeremy, at least once, the future) only as they appear to him. The doctor of *Nightwood* is not the spokesman for Miss Barnes; he is the spokesman for the doctor. In *The Antiphon*, the characters can be *seen* (which should make perception easier) to be speaking for themselves. The only real confusion is the mixing of identities between Augusta and Miranda: a confusion the characters suffer, more than the reader or audience. We are able to witness the costume change, the third-act transformation of Augusta as she becomes more girlish and fanciful; we hear the charges and accusations, the counter-charges and retaliations behind which the characters struggle to come to terms with their own perceptions of what they are, and of what their lives have been. The dramatic vehicle, because it presents at least a "kind" of reality, releases the poet from the necessity of verbalizing the mundane. The mechanics of drama, then, make the pursuit of a "pure" poetry more possible.

VI *Poetic Language*

What we find in *The Antiphon*, however, is not a single, unified poetry. Rather, two levels of poetry exist. The poetic "voice" which invests the play is shaped to the various characters, so that each has his own manner of speaking; but, at the same time, a consistent poetic "texture" is sustained. Jonathan Burley does not talk like Miranda; Miranda and Augusta have distinctive "voices"; Jeremy, a disguised character, disguises his speech by assuming a deliberately clownish or riddling manner. Even Dudley and Elisha have their own poetic language. Dudley's language is driving, direct, strongly motivated, and overbearing. Elisha, who tends to take his direction from Dudley, has less of his brother's strong purpose; he fragments his speech; and, when he appears strongest, he "echoes" Dudley. Jonathan, an elderly, ineffectual caretaker of a crumbling world, is mild in both his manners and his speech. His language is less ostentatious than that of Dudley and Elisha, or of Augusta, who likes to talk and shows it. At one point, she insists upon describing Victoria, her mother-in-law; and she evidently relishes doing so.

Miranda's language, which is the most compressed of all the characters, reflects a personality which has accustomed itself, through discipline, to silence. Miranda, who maintains a strictly "professional" relationship to the world, speaks as an actress or as a writer would in the voices of characters. Her dark view of existence causes her to appear to herself as a "victim" of life; and only death can rectify any injustice. What then, is there to talk about? Miranda often has to be goaded to speech. And yet to her is given the best poetry of the play, as though Barnes wishes to suggest that her "hard-won" silence has indeed paid off artistically.

Many differences, then, can be seen in the speeches of the characters since each voices his thoughts in a poetic language that arises from his own subjective nature. Yet, when considering these differences in speech dictated by the nature of the characters themselves, we are impressed by a poetic language that is common to all the characters and is elegant and archaic, unusual and apt. While many critics and reviewers identify the language as Jacobean, it is closer to being Shakespearean but with a metaphysical use of metaphor and simile that hearkens to John Donne. Indeed, part of the difficulty encountered in reading *The Antiphon* arises from the unusual and strained use of metaphor and from the rapid succession of apparently unrelated figures:

> Not so fast. It's true the webbed commune
> Trawls up a wrack one term was absolute;
> Yet corruption in its deft deploy
> Unbolts the caution, and the vesper mole
> Trots down the wintry pavements of the prophet's head.[10]

Miranda uses the archaic "wrack" for "wreck," and she follows the image of trawling (reinforced by "webbed," as in a net) with an image from land—and probably domestic—life: an unbolted "caution," a partially realized door image, through which emerges an underground animal. The mole is probably a figure for Miranda herself, even a figure for Miranda goaded to speech. But a "vesper mole" must be one that emerges at vespers, at the call of the church bell as evening draws on. Thus even in the compressed language of this small figure, the larger theme of the antiphon is not forgotten: one must respond.

Titus, like Wendell before him, failed at just this point. Both were forced by social pressures to break up their homes—to choose between a wife and a mistress. Wendell could not choose; Titus "recanted." Both betrayed their natures. But the vesper mole "Trots down the wintry pavement of the prophet's head"; emerges, that is, into the halls of Burley, which, like a prophetic "head," (suggestive of fatherhood), had foretold from the beginning the corruption and the doom to which, in all cases, life is addressed. For Titus had begun his "practice" while still at Burley: he had shaped his affairs into a brawl of "wives," and his children would total in theirs the sum of his life. As "mole," Miranda chooses to face what Titus could not. She rejects the easy accolade of Jack Blow's applause; Miranda will not be consoled at the expense of the truth. Like answering the vesper bell or responding to the antiphon, the bell of the called response, Miranda will face her life.

Richard Eberhart, who distinguishes between what he calls an inner and an outer verse drama, uses *The Antiphon* to illustrate the inner and MacLeish's *J. B.* to represent the outer verse drama. In outer verse drama, plot and action are paramount, and the author is scarcely concerned with style; rather, his verbal devices are simple but efficient enough to expedite the telling of his story. The reverse is true of inner verse drama, where richness of language is more important than plot or action; for the primary enjoyment is found in the language of the play: "the story, the problems of the play and their resolution, would constitute an essential but secondary awareness."[11] But the two forms, Eberhart contends, have never been combined successfully. The language of *The Antiphon* is so difficult, says Eberhart, that it is beyond even good readers and would slow down a lexicographer. The style, too, is overly difficult. Yet, after finding the play too esoteric, Eberhart concludes: "If the inverted world of Djuna Barnes' poetry is thistle and cockle, for all I know her eccentric diction may be timeless."[12]

The language of *The Antiphon* is demanding for two principal reasons. It is largely informed by the diction and vocabulary of Shakespeare, and it is, as well, metaphysical in its conceits. The strained, unusual metaphors, drawn from apparently unrelated sources, are demanding. Each line of the play must be analyzed as intensely as we unravel the meaning in a short, concise metaphysical poem. But the language of this play is made even more demanding by the author's evident indifference to the conventions of modern speech. *Nightwood*'s characters, despite the poetic language of its narrative portions, speak informally and even colloquially; the dialogue is direct; and figures of speech are familiar. The doctor's typical ejaculation is "Oh, for the love of God!" At one point he describes Nora as "beating her head against her heart, sprung over, her mind closing her life up like a heel on a fan, rotten to the bone for love of Robin."[13] While these are uniquely the doctor's own figures, they build upon modern colloquialisms. To "beat one's head against a wall," to "close up like a clamshell," or to be "rotten to the core" are familiar expressions that are adapted to serve more precisely the doctor's purposes.

If modern writers can be said to reflect their own age and to seek a style reasonably consonant with the colloquialisms, speech rhythms, and diction of their contemporaries, *Nightwood*'s characters speak a twentieth-century language. *The Antiphon* presents a real reversal of expectation, for Miss Barnes implies the thesis that literature exists quite outside of time and the fashions of the moment. The language of fine literature, she seems to suggest, has nothing to do with colloquial speech; it may, in fact, be an absolute. Although the action of the play occurs in a modern world torn by World War II, the play's language suggests that the same characters could have existed in the same interrelationships at any time during the past four hundred years.

Three dimensions of this style can be shown to coexist: the modern, the Elizabethan, and the post-Elizabethan or Jacobean. Jack Blow predicts the future: "I expect to see myopic conquerors/With pebbled monocles and rowel'd heels"[14] This language is familiar to any reader of modern poetry, but the spelling of roweled as "rowel'd" seems to harken back to the Renaissance. When Jack adds, "In a damned and horrid clutch of gluttony,"[15] he uses hendiadys to intensify "clutch of gluttony," when either "damned" or "horrid" would do, or "damned, horrid clutch" would seem closer to modern diction. As words, both "horrid" and "clutch" (used as a noun) occur in Shakespeare with greater frequency than they do in modern literature. Indeed, "a clutch of gluttony" doesn't occur today; we might find "a *nest* of gluttony," but even "gluttony" would probably be replaced by "greed" or "avarice."

The post-Elizabethan quality of *The Antiphon* is best suggested through the plot machinations of Dudley: "Our deadly beloved vixen, in the flesh./What more could two good brothers want?"[16] As he shapes his murderous plans to include Miranda, Dudley evinces the diabolical irony of Shakespeare's Iago, or of John Webster's conspirators in *The Duchess of Malfi.* Webster's play with its murderous intrigues resembles act 2 of *The Antiphon* in which the brothers figure. The structure of the play thus confounds encapsulation. When Dudley enters Burley with his watch in hand, his open umbrella is raised like a figure from a Harold Pinter "absurdist" play. He appears "absurd," which is to say symbolic; and we "read" his appearance to achieve its intended meaning. The same Dudley also recalls the post-Elizabethan theater when "effects" and surface drama—action—supplant an interest in characterization. The brothers are not individualized; they are cowardly conspirators, "bad guys." Act 3 relies much less on plot and plotters and more on character and personality differences between Augusta and Miranda, both of whom are individualized. Mother and daughter are less symbols, much more characters; their preoccupation with identity and their "influence" upon each other's lives is distinctly modern. The diction also changes, for the purpose of the playwright is far more inward looking, more profoundly concerned with the individualizing or personal aspects of human destiny. Miranda voices thoughts that the brothers are incapable of in a language that is beyond their reach.

Although demanding, *The Antiphon* is dramatically unified and sound. There is no question that it "works"—in fact, it did work successfully at the Royal Dramatic Theater of Stockholm, where it premiered to bewildered but enthusiastic audiences in a translation by the late Dag Hammarskjöld and Karl Ragnar Gierow.

CHAPTER 8

Conclusion

As Western man rushes toward the twenty-first century and whatever destiny he faces, it is apparent to many that writers of the twentieth century have had an extremely uneasy task. Their position, whether they like it or not, has been transitional; and they have shown their awareness of the past when the change was slow and hopeful. They have looked back at that past with every kind of response: they have been nostalgic, hurt, lost, angry, alienated; and some have even been persuaded that the future will be better. The twentieth-century artist, whatever his response, has been entrapped in change. Moreover, he has seen the abandonment, along the way, of the very forms that art once used, just as he has seen the rejection of the unhurried and relatively stable civilization that man once thought he was building. The artist who has experimented during this century has made both slight and radical changes. The pressures of his era have placed a premium on invention, so he has invented. As his world has fragmented, so has his art; and he has often found himself bemusedly putting together odds and ends, pieces of the past, arranged as montages and collages; and all glued together with impressionistic fury.

Whatever the twenty-first century holds, its artists will not be able to look back to the previous century with nostalgia for lost certainties. Those will be vanishing into the mists through which we presently view the age of Enlightenment, and the Declaration of Independence. Too far in the past to be easily related to by some modern authors, the nineteenth century's conventional linearly plotted and heavily characterized novels seem much less operable than do the fragmented forms of William Faulkner's *Sound and the Fury*, John Dos Passos's *U.S.A.*, Joyce's *Ulysses*, and Barnes's *Ryder*. Although the concept of the novel has been reestablished, the underlying ideas are not the once familiar ones. The conventions of the novel are now what the word itself has always implied: something new, a novelty. Most of the tinkering that has occurred in our century has been with style, form, structure, and meaning that are addressed to questions no one has ever succeeded in answering: what is a novel? What is it supposed to do? How is it put together? What are its limits? These questions have been answered repeatedly with new definitions; but the latest definition is usually refuted by a still more recent experimental work. Fiction, then, has evolved during the present century into a technical field. The novel, for example, sits there—an idea—endlessly experimented with; and the one injunction is that, since it does evolve, the serious artist may not settle for a previously established concept; he may not merely copy; he must continually reinvent the novel.

This study of Miss Barnes's works has tried to stress three considerations: her consistently naturalistic vision, and her almost unpredictable explorations with form and with style. Beginning early in this century with fictional tales narrated in the linear mode perfected in the nineteenth century by Poe and Hawthorne, she established a name for herself as a writer of short stories. Under the influence of the highly charged atmosphere found in the Paris of the 1920s, and enthusiastic about the newest work of such friends as T. S. Eliot, Ezra Pound, and James Joyce, she abandoned formulas to create her own. This determination did not carry with it any implicit promise that a new form or new style, once devised, could then be used again and again. Indeed, the reverse was true; invention could never cease. No form and no style could be repeated since repetition would merely signify that Barnes had ceased to struggle for the artistic revolution in progress. In rapid succession, she produced two startlingly fresh novels, both of which showed her concern for contemporary issues: *Ryder* challenged what are now called "establishment" values by contrasting the Ryder family's hedonistic life style with the tepid but "respectable" social institutions to which social man has consigned his freedoms. *Ladies Almanack*, on the other hand, urged a sensible restraint against self-indulgence in the liberated Paris of the 1920s, but it celebrated at the same time the lesbian coterie it appeared to scold. As has been shown, both works used older forms and even vocabularies, as well as freshly coined words, in new and inventive ways.

Nightwood, Miss Barnes's only sally into the field of the popular novel (*Ryder* had been published in a limited first edition of only three thousand copies), again revealed the author's sympathies with those alienated from their society. This time she examined an almost unknown night world whose central character, Robin, seems to embody the very antithesis of the reasoned, time-structured, daylight world. Stylistically, she adapted colloquial language to the needs of her characters; and she produced, out of the clichés of daily speech, a fresh and poetic language. As has been shown, her achievements with form in that novel are still being studied for their artistry. In *Nightwood*, Miss Barnes managed simultaneously to tell a tale in the traditional chronological order while at the same time, through the device of three chapters all of which end at the exact same point of time in the tale (the night Nora saw Jenny clinging to Robin in the garden), she seems to have employed the space-time relationships of what Sharon Spencer calls the Architectonic novel.[1]

In *The Antiphon*, Miss Barnes's exasperation with the modern world achieved its profoundest expression. In defiance of modern values, she sought the most archaic language to be found and created with it a poetry of such density and opaqueness as to guarantee the play's popular failure—only the most dedicated of her readers even attempt to fathom the work—while she assured its success as a demonstration of her power over language. For her dramatic structure, she also looked backward and used Elizabethan diction and Jacobean skullduggery to show the modern world that it has neither true values nor permanence. Miranda, artist and actress, is all too well aware of the condition of her world; and she can only counsel man to live up to the values he once set for himself: to respond to the vesper bell's call. But all her intent is in vain; for, in the world of global war, the family of man is itself hopelessly divided; and the artist too must perish.

Miss Barnes's themes have consistently taken the modern world to task, but her techniques reflect her careful study of the past. She has been influenced in diction and vocabulary by the Bible, Chaucer, Shakespeare, Donne, Milton, Fielding; by the literature of Manners, Sterne, and Joyce. With some justice, we may state that she has also admired these writers and their works for structural reasons. From the start of her longer work, she became an experimenter with fictional forms which tend to fragment, superimpose, juxtapose, or intertwine her thematic and plot lines. The episodic character of both her early and later models appears in the "spatial" quality or unorthodox arrangement of her material into forms which resist the linear-as-chronological schema typical of fictional narratives.

As suggested in chapter 6, I am not entirely persuaded as to the novelty of her structure. The picaresque novel, a very old form, is both episodic and susceptible to rearrangements of time; and certain chapters recount events occurring during the same time as other events described in previous chapters. A clearer sense of Barnes's purpose is obtained by considering time thematically rather than structurally. As interested in time rearrangements as she may be, Miss Barnes is much more interested in time as it relates to the degenerating patterns of Western society. She does not write, at the expense of theme, for the sake of creating poetic language; for both theme and style are important for her creation of her desired effect.

In turn, later writers, particularly those noted less for their popularity than for their craftsmanship, appear to have been influenced in varying degrees by Barnes's writings. For example, Faulkner showed evidence that we have indicated of having been influenced by Barnes as he sought to achieve the ideal of feminine beauty in his later novels, such as *The Hamlet*, *The Town* and *The Mansion*. Barnes is cited in the introduction to John Hawkes' novel *The Cannibal* as having influenced that writer stylistically, and Anais Nin's novels have been said to reflect such an influence.

As such conventions of the nineteenth century novel as its linear plot and its "realistic" characters are increasingly displaced by the challenges of our frighteningly changing times and people, we can anticipate that discerning readers as well as writers hopeful of improving their craftsmanship will turn in growing numbers to Miss Barnes's works for instruction.

Notes And References

Chapter One

1. Margaret Anderson, ed., *The Little Review Anthology* (New York: Hermitage House, Inc., 1953), p. 23. The final issue of the *Little Review* contained replies by contributors during the magazine's fifteen-year life to ten confessional questions ranging from likes and dislikes about oneself to questions about the world and the writers' attitudes toward life and art. Not all contributors polled chose to reply. One who replied, but chose not to answer the questions, was Miss Barnes, who wrote: "I am sorry but the list of questions does not interest me to answer. Nor have I that respect for the public." That was in 1929.

Chapter Two

1. "A Boy Asks A Question of a Lady," in *A Book* (New York: Boni & Liveright, 1923) p. 217.
2. "Aller et Retour," in *The Selected Works of Djuna Barnes* (New York: Farrar, Straus & Cudahy, 1962), p. 4. Hereafter cited as *Selected Works*.
3. Ibid., p. 9.
4. Ibid.
5. Ibid.
6. Ibid., p. 11.
7. "The Little Girl Continues" was also published in *Transition* and in the anthology *Americans Abroad* (The Hague, Holland, n.d.).
8. "Cassation," in *Selected Works*, p. 16.
9. Ibid., p. 18.
10. Ibid., p. 19.
11. Ibid., p. 20.
12. "The Grande Malade," in *Selected Works*, p. 20.
13. Ibid., p. 25.
14. "The Rabbit," in *Selected Works*, p. 51.
15. Ibid., p. 46.
16. "Katrina Silverstaff," in *A Book*, pp. 105–06.
17. Shakespeare, *Hamlet*, act 3, scene 1.
18. "Katrina Silverstaff," in *A Book*, p. 111.

Chapter Three

1. Floyd Dell, "Irrelevant," *The Nation* (Jan. 2, 1924), pp. 14–15.
2. Alexander Woollcott, "The Provincetown Plays," *New York Times* Nov. 9, 1919, section 8, p. 2.
3. "Three From the Earth," in *A Book*, p. 30.
4. Ibid., p. 25.
5. Ibid., p. 20.
6. Ibid., p. 24.
7. "To The Dogs," in *A Book*, p. 53.
8. "The Dove," in *A Book*, p. 153.
9. Ibid., pp. 157–58.
10. Ibid., p. 162.
11. Ibid., p. 162–63.
12. Ibid., p. 163.
13. Ibid.

Chapter Four

1. Robert McAlmon, *Being Geniuses Together* (London: Secker and Warburg, 1938), p. 168.
2. Ernest Hemingway, *The Sun Also Rises* (New York: Charles Scribner's Sons, 1954), p. 115.
3. McAlmon, *Being Geniuses Together*, p. 232.
4. Ibid., p. 232.
5. *Ryder* (New York: Liveright, 1928) p. 6.
6. Ibid., p. 18.
7. Ibid., p. 19.
8. Ibid., p. 26.
9. Ibid., p. 26–27.
10. Ibid., p. 36.
11. Ibid., p. 49.
12. Ibid., p. 53.
13. Ibid., p. 54.
14. Ibid., p. 57.
15. Ibid., p. 61.
16. Ibid., p. 70.
17. Ibid., p. 73.
18. Ibid., p. 146.
19. Ibid., p. 153.
20. Ibid., p. 156.
21. Ibid., p. 174.
22. Ibid., p. 174.
23. Ibid., p. 175–76.
24. Ibid., p. 177.

25. Ibid., p. 208.
26. Ibid., p. 231.
27. L.B., review of *Ryder*, *The New Republic* (Oct. 24, 1928), p. 282.
28. Review of *Ryder*, *The Nation* (Dec. 5, 1928), p. 639.
29. Ernest Sutherland Bates, review of *Ryder*, *Saturday Review* (Nov. 17, 1928), p. 376.

Chapter Five

1. Sylvia Beach, *Shakespeare and Co.* (New York: Harcourt, Brace and Co., 1956), p. 115.
2. Janet Flanner [Genêt], *Paris Was Yesterday: 1925–1939*, ed. Irving Drutman (New York: The Viking Press, 1972) p. xvii.
3. *Hamlet*, act 3, scene 2.

Chapter Six

1. Alan Williamson, "The Divided Image: The Quest for Identity in the Works of Djuna Barnes," *Critique: Studies in Modern Fiction*, 7 (1964), p. 68. [See pp. 58–74 inclusive.], describes this scene as patterned on Henri Rousseau's painting "The Dream" in which "a sleeping woman on a couch is transplanted from the real world of which she is oblivious, to the middle of a jungle, the world of her dream."
2. *Nightwood* (New York: Harcourt, 1961), p. 35.
3. Ibid., p. 40.
4. Ibid., p. 50.
5. Ibid., p. 63.
6. Ibid., p. 68.
7. Ibid., p. 67.
8. Ibid., p. 71.
9. Ibid., p. 73.
10. In *The Town* (New York: Random House, 1957; Vintage edition, 1961), p. 317, Faulkner makes this reference to *Ryder* in connection with Eula and her lover: "the spring which an American poet, a fine one, a woman and so she knows, called *girls' weather and boys' luck*" [italics mine]. *Nightwood*'s lioness, weeping self-consuming tears at the sight of Robin, evokes this parallel with Wallstreet Panic Snopes' wife in *The Town*, p. 148: "crying (weeping too but not tears, as if the fierce taut irreconcilable face blistered and evaporated tears away as fast as they emerged onto it) . . . ."

And Eula in Faulkner's *The Hamlet* (New York: Random House, 1959), p. 132, is very like our first sight of Robin: "among them the girl [Eula], the centrice here too—the body of which there was simply too much dressed in the clothing of childhood, [Robin characteristically wears boys' trousers] like a slumberer washed out of Paradise by a night flood and discovered by chance passers and covered hurriedly with the first garment to hand, still sleeping."

11. *Nightwood*, p. 79.
12. Ibid., p. 106.
13. Ibid., p. 107.
14. Ibid., p. 114.
15. Ibid., p. 116.
16. Ibid., p. 118.
17. Ibid., p. 121.
18. Ibid., p. 130. In the original, this reads "ladies of the *haute* sewer," but "sewer" is omitted in *Nightwood* as reprinted in *Selected Works*.
19. Ibid., p. 152.
20. Ibid., p. 156.
21. Ibid., p. 162.
22. Ibid., p. 166.
23. Ibid., p. 170.
24. Ibid.
25. Williamson, "The Divided Image," p. 74, sees this scene as more explicitly sexual: ". . . Robin, in an act which represents simultaneously a disintegration into total animality and a masochistic atonement for her guilt towards Nora, attempts intercourse with Nora's dog as Nora looks on horror-stricken." It scarcely needs pointing out that Robin is too dehumanized by now for guilt; that she is not shown as conscious that the dog belongs to Nora; that she is fully dressed.
26. Joseph Frank, "Crisis Mastery in Modern Literature," in *The Widening Gyre* (New Brunswick, N.J.: Rutgers University Press, 1963) pp. 29–30. [See pp. 25–49 inclusive.]
27. Ibid., p. 31–32.
28. Walter Sutton, "The Literary Image and the Reader: A Consideration of the Theory of Spatial Form," *Journal of Aesthetics and Art Criticism* 16 (Sept., 1957), 117. [See pp. 112–123 inclusive.]
29. Ibid., p. 120.
30. Jack Hirschman, "The Orchestrated Novel: A Study of Poetic Devices in Novels of Djuna Barnes, and Hermann Broch, and the Influences of the Works of James Joyce upon Them." (Ann Arbor: University Microfilms, Inc., 1961), pp. 110, 122–126.
31. Frank, *The Widening Gyre*, p. 32.
32. Ibid., p. 49.
33. Robert McAlmon, "Distinguished Air," in *McAlmon and the Lost Generation: A Self-Portrait*, ed. Robert E. Knoll (Lincoln, University of Nebraska Press, 1962), p. 222.
34. Ibid., p. 224.

35. Ibid. Elsewhere (p. 168) McAlmon wrote: "In her *Nightwood* [Miss Barnes] has a well-known character floundering in the torments of soul-probing and fake philosophies, and he just shouldn't. The actual person doubtlessly suffers enough without having added to his character this unbelievable dipping into the deeper meanings. Drawn as a wildly ribald and often broadly funny comic he would emerge more impressively."

36. *Nightwood*, p. 92.

37. Radclyffe Hall, *The Well of Loneliness* (New York: Covici Friede, 1929), p. 437.

38. Peggy Guggenheim claims to have met the original of Robin at a party mentioned in *Out of This Century* (New York: Dial Press, 1946), p. 33: "Later I received a proposal (I can hardly say of marriage) from the girl who was to become the well known Robin of *Nightwood*. She got down on her knees in front of me."

Chapter Seven

1. *The Antiphon*, in *Selected Works*, p. 114.
2. Ibid., p. 130.
3. Ibid., p. 140.
4. Shakespeare, *Hamlet*, act 5, scene 1.
5. *The Antiphon*, in *Selected Works*, p. 203.
6. Djuna Barnes, "Crystals," *The New Republic*, 35, no. 446 (June 20, 1923), 101.
7. *The Antiphon*, in *Selected Works*, p. 223.
8. *The Little Review Anthology*, ed. Margaret Anderson. Anderson quotes from Richard Aldington's letter to the *Little Review* (New York, 1953), p. 23. (Summer, 1915), but these tenets were originated by Ezra Pound.
9. "Antique," in *A Book*, p. 103.
10. *The Antiphon*, in *Selected Works*, p. 83.
11. Richard Eberhart, "Outer and Inner Verse Drama," *Virginia Quarterly Review*, 34, no. 4(Autumn 1958) 618. [See pp. 618–23 inclusive.]
12. Ibid., pp. 619, 623.
13. *Nightwood*, p. 161.
14. *The Antiphon*, in *Selected Works*, p. 91.
15. Ibid., p. 91.
16. Ibid., p. 99.

Chapter Eight

1. Sharon Spencer, *Space, Time and Structure in the Modern Novel* (New York: New York University Press, 1971).

Selected Bibliography

PRIMARY SOURCES

1. Books

The Book of Repulsive Women, 8 Rhythms and 5 Drawings. New York: [Guido] Bruno Chapbook, 1915. Reprinted as *Outcast Chapbook No. 14*. New York: Alicat Bookshop Press, 1948.

A Book. New York: Boni & Liveright, 1923.

Ryder. New York: Liveright, 1928.

Ladies Almanack. Dijon: Contact Editions, 1928.
Published privately and authored anonymously by "A Lady of Fashion." Reprinted, New York: Harper & Row, 1972.

A Night Among the Horses and Other Stories. New York: Liveright, 1929.

Nightwood. New York: Harcourt; London: Faber and Faber, 1937. Republished in London in 1950 by Faber and Faber; in New York by New Directions, as New Classic No. 11, 1946.

The Antiphon. New York: Farrar, Strauss; London: Faber and Faber, 1958.

The Selected Works of Djuna Barnes. New York: Farrar, Straus & Cudahy, 1962.

Spillway. London: Faber and Faber, 1962. New York: Harper & Row, 1972.

Vagaries Malicieux. New York: Frank Hallman, 1974.

2. Short Works

"Call of the Light." *Harpers* 55 (Dec. 23, 1911), 22.

"Antique." *Harpers*, 137 (August, 1918), 330.

"A Night Among the Horses." *Little Review* 5, no. 8 (1918), 3–10.

"Finale." *Little Review* 5, no. 2 (1918), 29–30.

"The Lament of Women: Ah My God!" *Little Review* 5, no. 8 (1918), 37.

"Three From the Earth." *Little Review* 6, no. 7 (1919), 3–15.

"The Valet." *Little Review* 6, no. 1 (1919), 3–9.

"Beyond the End." *Little Review* 6, no. 8 (1919), 7–14.

"To the Dead Favorite of Liu Ch'e." *Dial* 68 (April, 1920), 444.

"Pastoral." *Current Opinion* 69 (August, 1920), 268; *Dial*, 68 (April, 1920), 445–46.

"Oscar." *Little Review* 6, no. 11 (1920), 7–23.
"Mother." *Little Review* 7, no. 2 (1920), 10–14.
"The Robin's House." *Little Review* 7, no. 3 (1920), 31–38.
"Katrina Silverstaff." *Little Review* 7, no. 4 (1921), 27–33.
"Crystals." *New Republic* 35 (June 20, 1923), 101.
"First Communion." *Dial* 75 (August, 1923), 166.
"Dusie." In *American Esoterica*. New York: Macy-Masois, 1927. Privately published.
"The Quarry." *The New Yorker* 45 (Dec. 27, 1969), 53.
"The Walking-Mort." *The New Yorker* 47 (May 15, 1971), 34.

3. Articles

"Reader Critic." *Little Review* 8, no. 2, (1922), 35.
"Confessions-Questionnaire." *Little Review* 12, no. 2 (1929), 17.

BIBLIOGRAPHY

HIPKISS, ROBERT. "Djuna Barnes (1892–): A Bibliography." *Twentieth Century Literature* 24, no. 3 (October, 1968), 161–63.

SECONDARY SOURCES

1. Background Books

GUGGENHEIM, PEGGY. *Out of This Century*. New York: Dial Press, 1946. This autobiography has numerous references to the author's friendship with Miss Barnes.

MCALMON, ROBERT. *Being Geniuses Together*. London: Secker and Warburg, 1938. Penetrating observations of the Paris of the 1920s; it has several allusions to Miss Barnes.

———. *McAlmon and the Lost Generation: A Self-Portrait*. Edited by Robert E. Knoll. Lincoln: University of Nebraska Press, 1962. Helpful in clarifying certain aspects of the nightlife of Europe during the time covered in *Nightwood*.

2. Reviews and Articles

EBERHART, RICHARD. "Outer and Inner Verse Drama." *Virginia Quarterly Review* 34 (1958), 618–23. Eberhart distinguishes between "outer verse drama like "J. B.," in which MacLeish sacrifices poetry to plot, and *The Antiphon*, an "inner" verse drama in which plot is sacrificed to poetic intensity.

FRANK, JOSEPH. "Spatial Form in Modern Literature: Miss Barnes' *Nightwood*." *Sewanee Review* 53 (1945), 433–56. Reprinted as "Crisis Mastery in Modern Literature" in Frank's *The Widening Gyre*. New Brunswick, N.J.: Rutgers University Press, 1963. Good discussion of the generation of spatial form, together with an application of the theory, using *Nightwood* for illustration.

HIRSCHMAN, JACK A. "The Orchestrated Novel: A Study of Poetic Devices in the Novels of Djuna Barnes and Hermann Broch and the Influences of the Works of James Joyce Upon Them." Ph.D. dissertation, Indiana University, 1961; Ann Arbor: University Microfilms, Inc., 1961. Helpful and intelligent review of Miss Barnes's early work and analysis of *Nightwood* as "orchestrated" novel. Tends, however, to press musical analogies too far and into realms of unsupported speculation.

HYMAN, STANLEY E. "The Wash of the World." *Standards: A Chronicle of Books For Our Time*. New York: Horizon Press, 1966. An English teacher's reappraisal of *Nightwood* as a novel that stands the test of time.

PONSOT, MARIE. "Careful Sorrow and Observed Compline." *Poetry* 95 (October, 1959), 47–50. Sympathetic, admiring review of *The Antiphon;* particular emphasis on the play's richness of language.

SUTTON, WALTER. "The Literary Image and the Reader: A Consideration of the Theory of Spatial Form." *Journal of Aesthetics and Art Criticism* 16 (September, 1957), 112–23. Essentially a rebuttal to Frank's article, Sutton takes issue with the Spatial Form Theory; expresses a well-argued preference for a Poundian "Image Complex" approach to *Nightwood.*

WILLIAMSON, ALAN. "The Divided Image: The Quest for Identity in the Works of Djuna Barnes." *Critique: Studies in Modern Fiction* 7 (1964), 58–74. Most lucid discussion of Barnes's themes of identity in both *Nightwood* and *The Antiphon.*

Index

(The works of Barnes are listed under her name.)